ELBPHILHARMONIE

HAMBURG

EDEL

JOACHIM MISCHKE / MICHAEL ZAPF

ELBPHILHARMONIE

HAMBURG

CONTENTS

Outstanding architecture:
the Elbphilharmonie
crowns the western
reaches of HafenCity.

Prologue

The crown jewel of HafenCity.

The Elbphilharmonie in the heart of Hamburg.

Worth seeing, from any side.

The lovely newcomer: the Elbphilharmonie's glass facade fits in with its surroundings, offering a virtuoso play of light and shadow.

A role model: even as the HafenCity district was emerging, the Elbphilharmonie was already visible, the most distinctive building at the western end of the new district.

Mixed doubles:
a longstanding Hamburg
landmark—St. Michaelis—
reflected in the facade of
its newest landmark.

World Heritage Site meets modern
cultural icon: there is a strong
aesthetic contrast between the
historic brick-built Speicherstadt and
the Elbphilharmonie's glass facade.

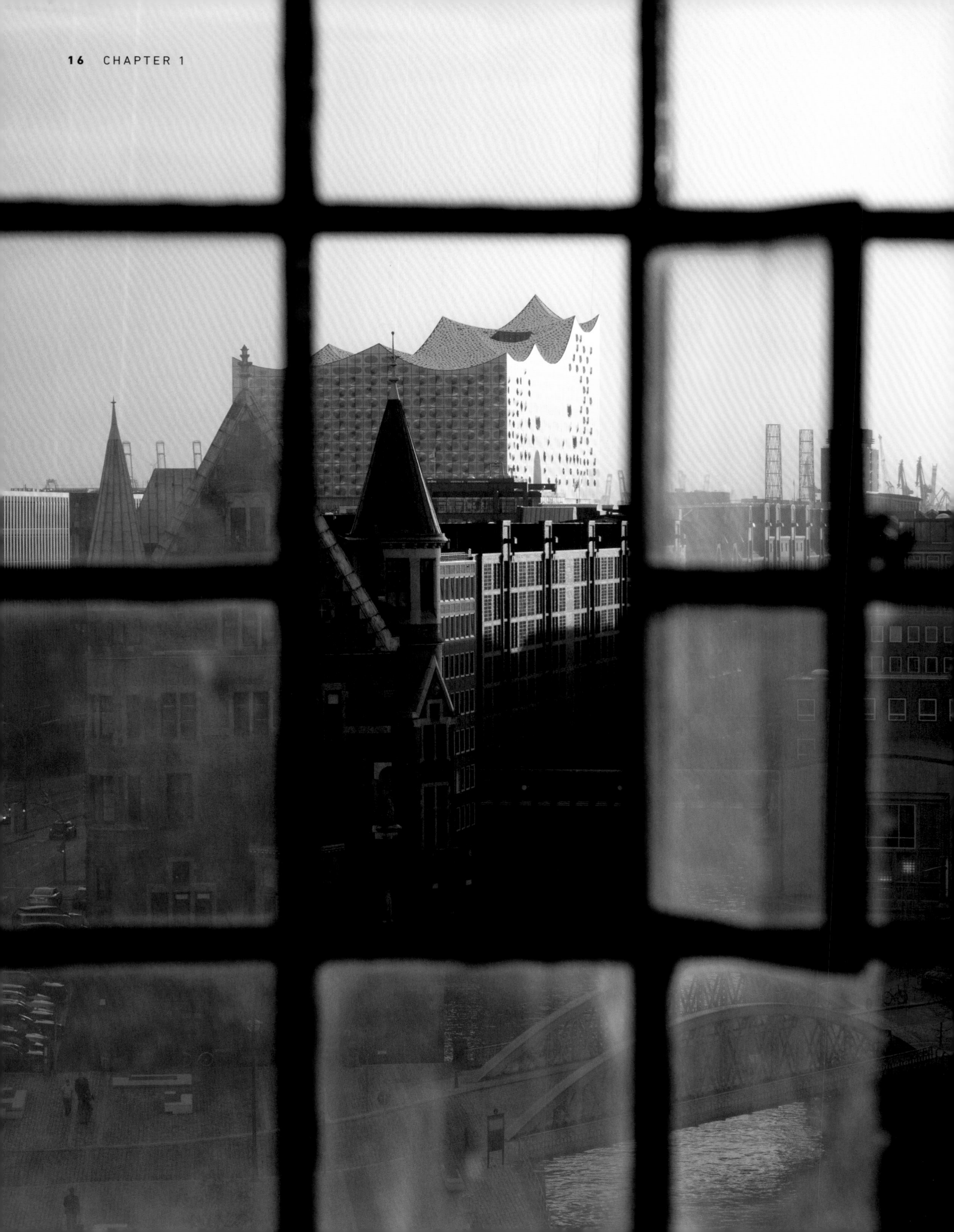

GATEWAY TO THE WORLD

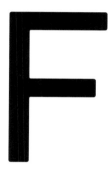

From the moment the music begins until the silence that falls before the final burst of applause, the rest of the world remains just that: the rest of the world. Every concert in the Elbphilharmonie has the potential to be a life-changing moment for the people in the audience. The concert hall sits in a fantastic location in the heart of the city that is also its emotional centre, because it was here that Hamburg sought, and dared to achieve, something extraordinary. The Elbphilharmonie tells the story of the Hanseatic city and is also its future. This building is a creation from which Hamburg as a whole, as a citywide community, benefits enormously—in all respects, not just financially. With the emergence of HafenCity on the banks of the River Elbe, the city is writing a new chapter in its history, and the Elbphilharmonie is the outstanding example of this transformation. Rising above the waves, it sends ripples across the globe.

The concert hall has now become an integral visual element of the port, no less iconic than the barge tours that chug regularly through the Elbe's waters. When the sun is out, the Elbphilharmonie sparkles like a diamond. If the sky darkens, so does the building's glass facade; in these moments, its metallic grey has a cool, dramatic effect. Shimmering or cool, it certainly leaves no one cold in this city, where it has inspired strong feelings from the very start. Where, despite every price-hike, every delay, every curse uttered during a crisis phase, construction always resumed, albeit reluctantly. Where the love affair with the Elbphilharmonie began.

A musical seed is embedded in the building's soul. It came about because a Hamburg couple, Alexander Gérard and Jana Marko, wanted, as culture lovers, to believe that something like this was possible in their city. It acts as a reminder that Hamburg's exceptional musical tradition extends back in time for centuries, populated by many famous composers. The golden age of the Baroque. Handel's apprenticeship at the Oper am Gänsemarkt. Georg Philipp Telemann, Carl Philipp Emanuel Bach. Birthplace of Johannes Brahms, of Felix and Fanny Mendelssohn. The motor of Gustav Mahler's career. The Beatles, the Star-Club. The adopted home of György Ligeti, Alfred Schnittke and Sofia Gubaidulina. The Reeperbahn Festival. And, now, the site of the Elbphilharmonie. Rising to a height of 110 metres on the HafenCity's western tip, it is also a high-rise, not because of its dimensions, but because it strives to project itself far beyond the city's horizon. It has goals. And it is this that has altered Hamburg beyond recognition.

After the Second World War, architect Werner Kallmorgen was instrumental in the reconstruction of the Speicherstadt, the largest warehouse district in the world, on the banks of the River Elbe. It was Kallmorgen, too, who designed and built Kaispeicher A in the mid-1960s. Erected within sight of the St. Pauli Piers, the warehouse was intended to store, primarily, cocoa and coffee. This Kaispeicher, in turn, made obsolete by shifts in the sea-freight industry, became the foundation of the idea for the Elbphilharmonie, the base of the glassy wave above the waves of the Elbe. Swiss architects Jacques Herzog and Pierre de Meuron have crowned HafenCity's western tip with this diadem. In June 2015, the Speicherstadt and the neighbouring Chilehaus were named UNESCO World Heritage Sites. The Elbphilharmonie already carries epochal significance for Hamburg. The contrast between old and new is what brings it to life and makes it so inspiring. Archetypal Hamburg brick acts as a reminder of the local yesterday, while attention-grabbing architecture acts as a global sign for tomorrow. And in between, the two are artfully fused: the Plaza, a wide open space meant for everyone, as big as the market square in front of Hamburg's City Hall. Open views over the harbour. A gateway to the world.

In the concert halls of the late 19th century, the walls are covered in ornamentation that redirects sound and, moreover, is a source of visual distraction. In the Grand Hall of the Elbphilharmonie, however, the architecture foregrounds the essence of the place. The walls are lined with what appear to be diagrammatic sound waves frozen in clay. That is the only 'ornament' to speak of. This delicate-looking 'white skin' is made of individually moulded gypsum fibre panels—extremely precise work. To it, the hall owes its excellent sound which, together with the architecture of the building, makes it the most important and boldest concert hall in existence today.

The rough 'white skin' contains a subtle message. Its waves seem to say: what we look like is not important. We serve the music. The room places the music at its centre, in every sense of the word. It stands in the middle of a community that, by entering this space, has agreed to define music as an essential cultural asset. The Grand Hall, the grand chamber of the heart, has massive proportions—and feels as intimate as if it were a performance space for chamber music. Not one of the nearly 2,100 audience members is more than 30 metres from the conductor.

At the turn of the millennium, Ole von Beust, then Hamburg's First Mayor, recognized a historic opportunity and pounced on it. Christoph Lieben-Seutter remembers: 'I was summoned to lead the greatest concert hall in the world. I came, and I found a big hole.' Hailing from Vienna and appointed general director in 2007, he had to wait quite a bit longer than originally expected for the opening concert in January 2017 in the new building with the NDR Elbphilharmonie Orchester and principal conductor Thomas Hengelbrock. Olaf Scholz was the third and final head of local government during the history of the construction project. Scholz and his Culture Senator Barbara Kisseler made its completion possible.

'The whole world will come,' prophesied Hamburg's general music director Kent Nagano in the spring of 2016, speaking of a building with no parallel in the world of music. The Elbphilharmonie is a dream that, nevertheless, came true. That was able to come true precisely because it was dreamed in the first place.

A direct view of the Elbphilharmonie, looking across from the Marco-Polo-Terrassen in HafenCity.

Dawn breaks: sunlight turns
the eastern facade into a vast
palette of colours.

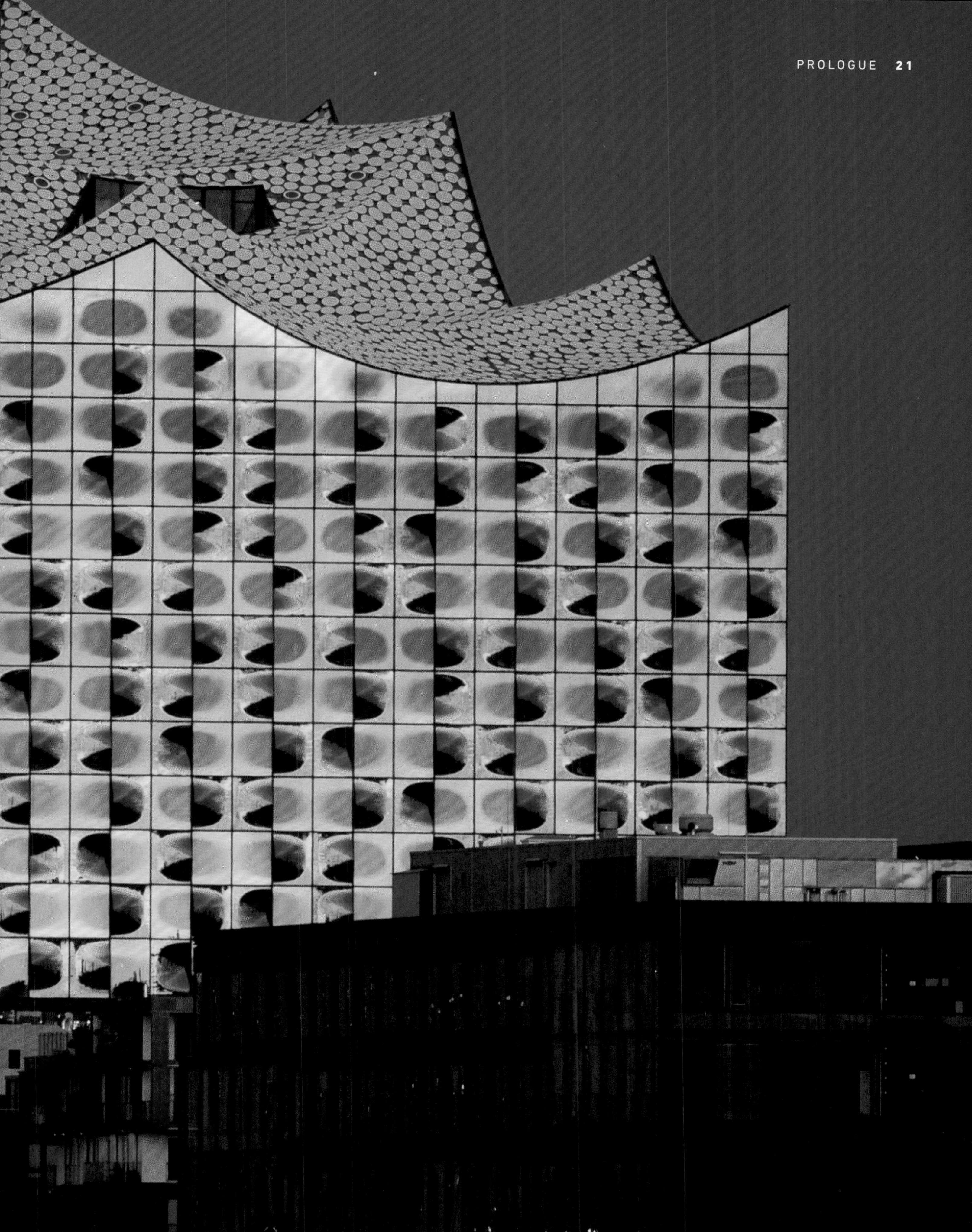

The Magellan-Terrassen are a popular meeting spot in HafenCity.

July 2016: the first open-air
concert of the NDR Elbphilharmonie
Orchester featuring cellist Sol
Gabetta at the Baakenhafen,
an area with a view of the
neighbouring Elbphilharmonie,
was a foretaste of the future
performances at the new concert
hall.

Reaching far into the Hamburg
sky: the crests of the glass waves
on the building's western side.

'Out from St. Pauli Piers / A view deserving cheers.'
The mood of these lines, by Hamburg band Kettcar,
perfectly suits the evening view from an apartment
on the building's west side.

Soundscape: the harbour and the Elbe
define the setting of the concert house.
The terrace surrounds the Plaza, offering
visitors the possibility of walking the
entire perimeter of the Elbphilharmonie
and views in every direction.

Above: good neighbours: the museum ship Cap San
Diego is at anchor at the Überseebrücke.
Left: a monumental view of the Elbphilharmonie Plaza.

St. Michaelis on the left, in the centre the Elbphilharmonie, on the right the television tower: three famous Hamburg buildings, here seen from Kamerunkai in the south-western port.

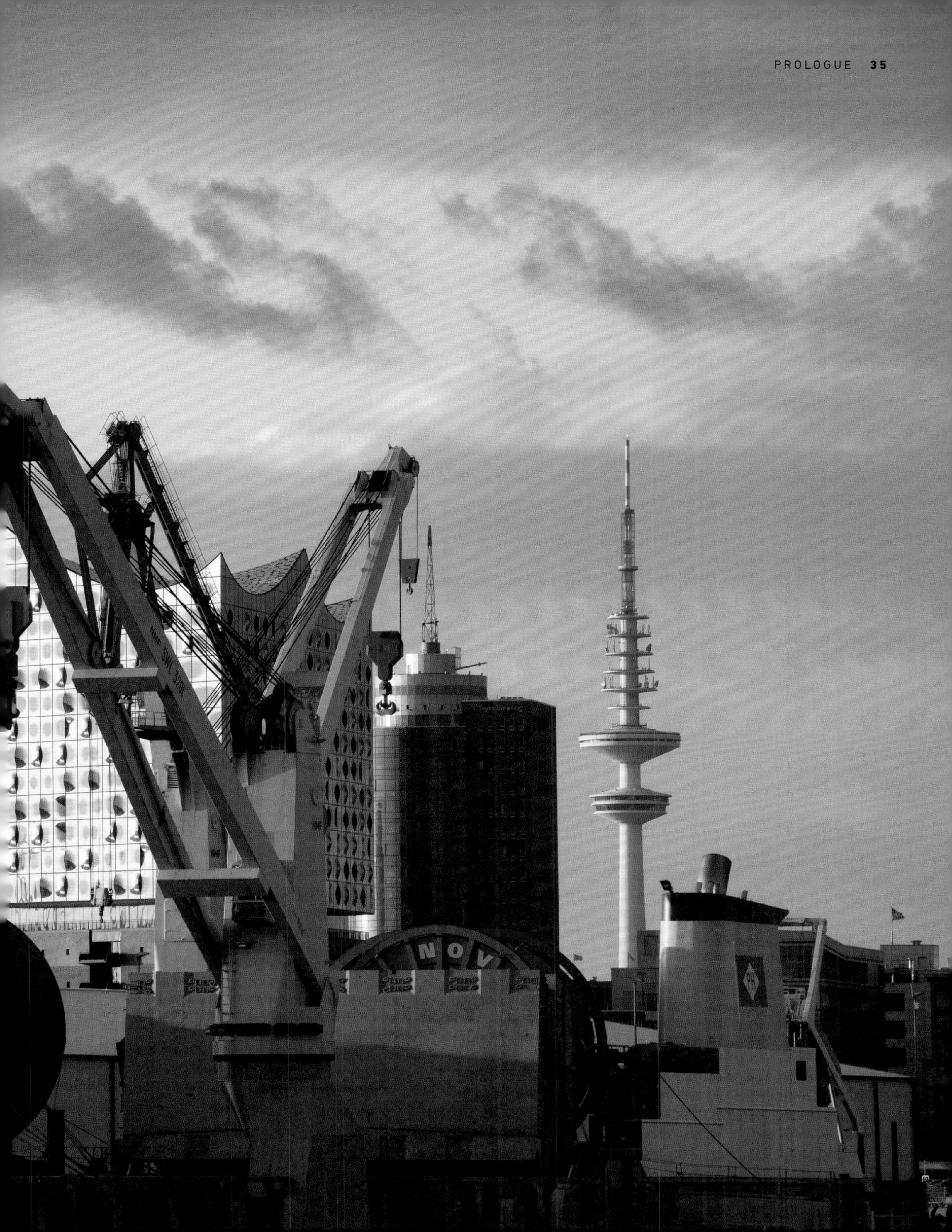
NOV

Above: the three-masted barque 'Rickmer Rickmers' and
some barges at the St. Pauli Piers.
Left: a view of politics and culture: Hamburg City Hall and the
Elbphilharmonie seen in a single glance. In the foreground,
the Alster Fountain.

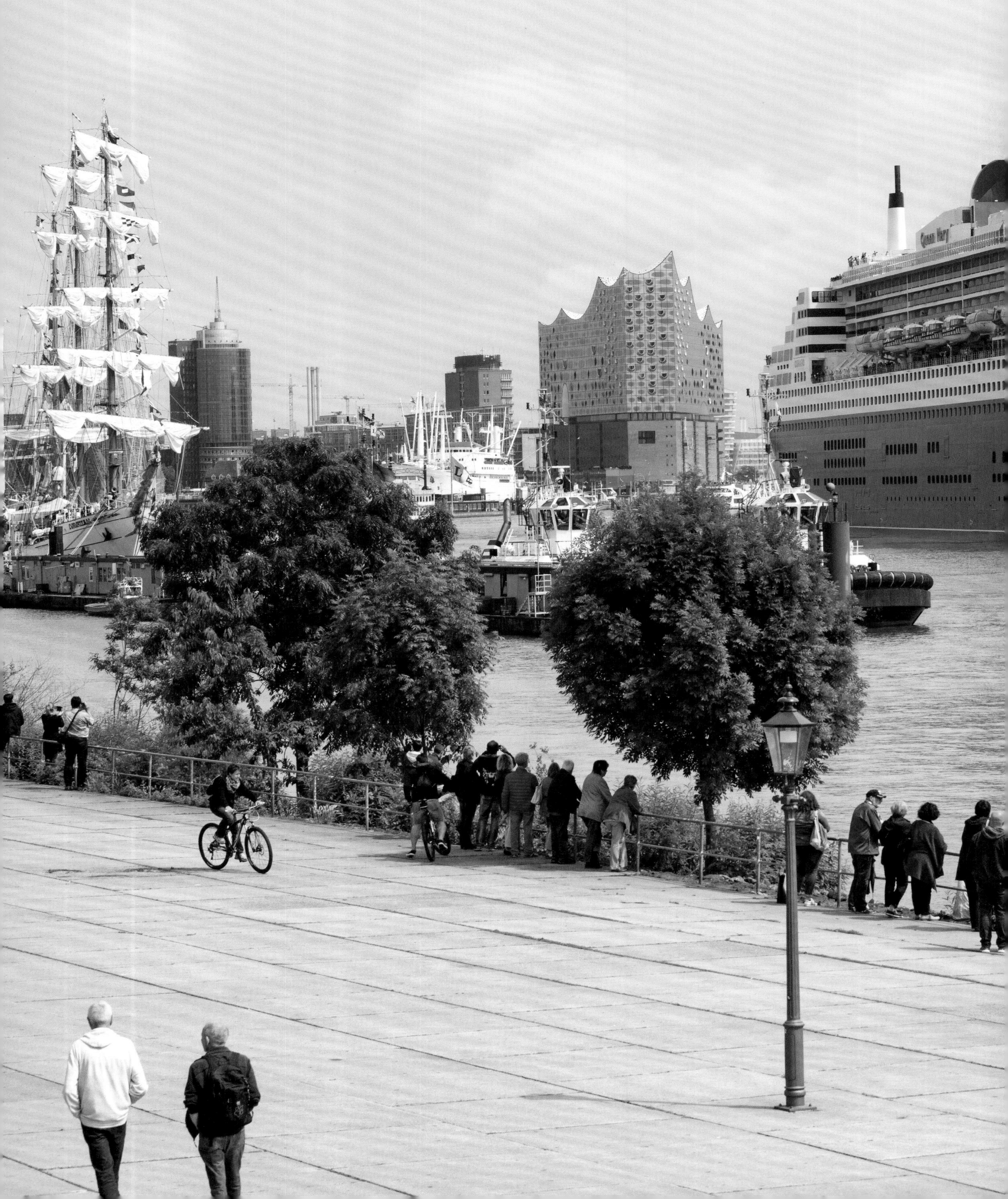

The 'Queen Mary 2' leaves the port of Hamburg, watched by sightseers.

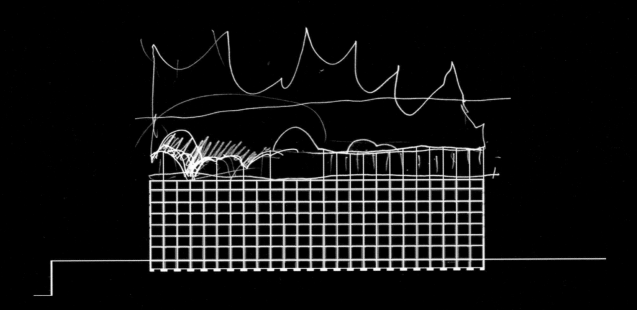

2

Genesis

The overture first takes shape as a rough sketch.

An idea that immediately catches people's imagination.

Optimistic plans encounter hefty opposition.

A historic opportunity for the city is finally grasped.

The foundations of the Elbphilharmonie are laid,
and with them the seeds of future problems.

HERZOG & DE MEURON
THE ARCHITECTS

Jacques Herzog and Pierre de Meuron opened their office in Basel in 1978. Today, the firm is managed by its founders and by senior partners Christine Binswanger, Ascan Mergenthaler and Stefan Marbach. An international team of 380 works on projects throughout Europe, Asia and America. In addition to the Basel headquarters, there are offices in Hamburg, London, New York and Hong Kong. Herzog & de Meuron were named the 2001 laureates by the Pritzker Architecture Prize (the Nobel Prize of architecture) in recognition of their body of built work. And in point of fact, their designs are by and large spectacular. Whether they are busy envisioning the Allianz Arena in Munich or the National Stadium (Bird's Nest) in Beijing, Herzog & de Meuron's recipe for success remains the same: no ready-made buildings, only unique structures custom-made for their surroundings. Like London's Tate Modern. Or the Elbphilharmonie—the first outline of which, so the story goes, was sketched with quick strokes directly onto a photograph of Kaispeicher A during a meeting with project initiators Alexander Gérard and Jana Marko.

Pictured are Jacques Herzog (left) and Pierre de Meuron (right) with Ascan Mergenthaler, the senior partner responsible for the Elbphilharmonie project, during construction of the Grand Hall.

'THE ELBPHILHARMONIE INCLUDES A PUBLIC SPACE OVERLOOKING THE ROOFTOPS OF HAMBURG. THAT WAS IMPORTANT TO US.'

PIERRE DE MEURON — ARCHITECT

2001–2017

ELBPHILHARMONIE THROUGH THE YEARS

How a new concert hall grew out of a warehouse and an idea.

31 OCTOBER

OCTOBER 2001   NOVEMBER 2001

Alexander Gérard's partner Patrick Taylor writes a letter to First Mayor Ole von Beust, suggesting the renovation of the Kaispeicher into a concert hall.

nce upon a time there was a warehouse. It stood directly on the banks of the River Elbe in one of Hamburg's best locations. Inside, the smell of cocoa hung in the air and the offices were piled high with furniture. Those granted access to its dusty interior soon felt that there was really nothing to be done with the building—abandoned and neglected, it seemed to have no relevance to the rest of the world. Located in the centre of the city of Hamburg, the old Kaispeicher A, or 'Wharf Warehouse A', stood like a relic of former times: too large to ignore, but also, due to its size, too large to convert into anything worthwhile.

That's the start of the fantastic story of the Elbphilharmonie. It began with an initial idea and a sketch—a spur-of-the-moment suggestion hastily drawn by Jacques Herzog on a photograph of the warehouse at a meeting in the library of an architecture firm in Basel on 21 December 2001: the crest of a wave rising upwards from the redbrick rectangle—daringly ambitious from the outset. The idea behind the sketch was massive and radical.

In recent decades, many large cities have invested in the construction of impressive cultural buildings, hoping to gain the competitive edge with an iconic eye-catcher. Noteworthy examples are the Spanish port city of Bilbao, where star-architect Frank Gehry created a temple to the arts with his Guggenheim Museum, which has attracted tourists from all over the world ever since. Urban planners in Oslo saw investment in culture as a social necessity from which a modern community could benefit as a whole. This is how the new Oslo Opera House became a modern landmark. The new Philharmonie de Paris was deliberately situated outside of the city centre in order to bring the idea of music as one of life's staples to the outskirts of the French capital. Ideally, concert halls should fire the imagination of their visitors and increase our sense of well-being; they should be places where we can experience at first-hand the power that music can unleash.

21 DECEMBER

DECEMBER 2001   JANUARY 2002   FEBRUARY 2002

Alexander Gérard meets architects Jacques Herzog and Pierre de Meuron in Basel. The first drawing of the Elbphilharmonie is made.

ALEXANDER GÉRARD AND JANA MARKO
THE INITIATORS

Everything began with them. He: New York-born, educated as an architect in Zurich. A reserved, sophisticated fellow who has successfully served as a project developer for the Hanseatic Trade Center, among others. She: born in Linz, Austria, an art historian, sparkling with energy and creativity. A pair with vision—and the drive to turn it into reality. Alexander Gérard and Jana Marko recognized the potential contained in Kaispeicher A, brought architects Jacques Herzog and Pierre de Meuron on board, and advocated, even fought for their idea in Hamburg. No one can take this achievement away from them, despite the fact that Gérard and Marko left the project team in 2004; the Elbphilharmonie is and remains their idea.

Project initiators Alexander Gérard and Jana Marko wanted the Hamburg concert hall they envisioned to be accordingly spectacular. Their idea was to use an existing building, surrounded on three of its four sides by water, as a pedestal. Rising 37 metres from the water, a complex building with many different functions and, at its centre, the grand concert hall, nestled within a hotel and apartments. And a plaza open to the public, where everyone can enjoy the amazing panoramic views of Hamburg, even if they haven't booked a room in the hotel, a table in the restaurant, or a ticket for the concert hall. And why stop there? Why not add a few dozen private apartments on the western side, where no future developer can ever spoil the view of sunsets over the Elbe? How about a car park deep in the bowels of the building? And, as the pièce de résistance, why not encase the whole new structure in a high-tech glass facade, never before seen on this planet?

The intention is to equip the entire complex with all sorts of structural ingenuities, but the crowning glory will of course be the concert hall itself—its acoustics as excellent as the appearance of the building from which they originate. 'The Elbphilharmonie includes a public space overlooking the rooftops of Hamburg. That was very important to us,' Pierre de Meuron would explain later on. 'It's there for everyone and not just for the top one-per cent.' De Meuron went on to say: 'Like the needle in acupuncture, the arrival of the Philharmonie in the city will inject it with new energy!'

In the years that have passed since the initial idea, the plans for the exterior have changed as much as those for the interior. Yet the building itself has retained its considerable dynamism, due in part to the sheer breadth of its multiple functions and different sections, all incorporated in a location that could hardly be more fascinating. All this for a city—the only city of its size in Germany, that 'nation of culture'—that for decades has got by with just one concert hall dedicated to classical music.

Project developer Alexander Gérard and art historian Jana Marko decided they could no longer sit back and accept the 'powers that be' affecting Hamburg's cultural-political life. Inspired by a combination of local patriotism, international sophistication, curiosity and fierce determination, these two private individuals got the ball rolling, holding numerous behind-the-scenes meetings, and seeking allies for their cause. At the time, the Laeiszhalle was chronically over-stretched. The programme was quickly filled up with every municipal orchestra and touring star that wanted to play there, not to mention a stream of smaller ensembles. During the day there were rehearsals, the erecting and striking of stage sets; in the evening, concerts.

There was little room left for the Laeiszhalle to develop a programmatic profile. Official subsidies from the city only began in 2005. The Laeiszhalle was regarded throughout Europe as a reliable venue, but not a top-league one. It was essentially a stage for hire. Whoever wanted to could perform there, if they had the money. The most bizarre example was a Danish archivist who, believing he was an exceptionally gifted pianist, frequently rented the Main Hall at the Laeiszhalle in the nineties to show off his talents to whichever random guests happened to turn up on the night.

Anyone hoping to introduce something new is usually met with adversity. And whenever demands to change the situation at the Laeiszhalle grew louder, the troublemakers were quickly put in their place. The first director to try to turn his office into something more than an administrative post was Benedikt Stampa. The blows that he was dealt in various debates and disputes had at least one positive outcome— they smoothed the way in 2006 for Christoph Lieben-Seutter. Kaispeicher A on the western tip of HafenCity was familiar to Alexander Gérard from his time as a project developer and driving force behind the construction of the neighbouring Hanseatic Trade Center. Nonetheless, that it all came together

CONCERT HALLS ARE MUCH MORE than just an event venue with a roof. They are feelings realized in brick and mortar, home to moments of happiness; they are places to be delighted and transported. While the more historical, classical models from the bourgeois days of the 19th century often resemble and can easily be confused with museums both inside and out, in our day and age building a new concert hall has become a fascinating act of customized, precision work. They are erected in special places, and they also enrich those places architecturally. Starchitects have realized custom-made designs around the globe. The more eccentric the forms expressed and the materials used, the better.

HARPA, REYKJAVÍK

9 OCTOBER

OCTOBER 2002   NOVEMBER 2002   DECEMBER 2002

First Mayor Ole von Beust announces a 'cultural and architectural highlight' for Hamburg.

According to the initiators' initial calculation, construction of the Elbphilharmonie was to cost around €95 million.

the way it ultimately did was more down to coincidence than anything else. Coincidence number one: while studying architecture in Zurich, the New Yorker Alexander Gérard got to know the Swiss architects Jacques Herzog and Pierre de Meuron. The two had set up office in Basel in 1978 and rapidly made a name for themselves with exceptional projects all over the world. Partly because they are imaginative architects, but mostly because of their intuitive ability to grasp the true essence of a place, its history, its meaning and its potential as a public space. A building by Herzog & de Meuron only ever functions in the exact spot it was designed for. It cannot be simply transplanted or copied from A to B. It works because it was thoroughly planned in advance to fit its surroundings, designed for a specific purpose at a specific location.

At the Basel headquarters of Herzog & de Meuron, hundreds of people from all over the world pore over new concepts and projects. One team is preoccupied with philosophies of colour for buildings in India. Another is developing concepts for futuristic skyscrapers in New York. The portfolio of the renowned architects includes a Prada shop in Tokyo as well as the Allianz Arena in Munich and museums in Miami and San Francisco.

In 2001, Herzog & de Meuron were awarded the Pritzker Architecture Prize—considered the Nobel Prize of architecture—for their body of work. And their project Tate Modern, a refurbishment of a power plant on the banks of London's River Thames, became the largest and most spectacular museum for contemporary art in the world, a real crowd-puller and, in its own way, a forerunner of the Elbphilharmonie. In October of the same year—historical coincidence number two—after 44 years of social-democratic dominance in Hamburg's City Hall, the conservative politician Ole von Beust from Germany's Christian Democratic Union (CDU) was elected First Mayor of Hamburg. But there were few indications that the new Senate would support a new concert

hall, especially not on the site of Kaispeicher A. The property had been allocated to the Media City Port project, for offices for the media industry. At the end of October 2001, von Beust received a letter from Gérard's co-planner Patrick Taylor, in which he discussed the idea of using the warehouse as the base for a concert hall. City Hall rejected the proposal—the future of the property had already been decided.

But Alexander Gérard and Jana Marko weren't quite ready to give up yet. They travelled throughout Europe to gather expert opinions from specialists in the music sector on how to implement their concept. In December in Basel, Gérard recalled later, Jacques Herzog sketched his vision of the concert hall on a photo with rolling waves reaching towards the skies, declaring that it should look 'something like this'. However, during this phase of research and finding answers, Ole von Beust's Culture Senator Dana Horáková was toying with the idea of an 'AquaDome', a concert hall with an inbuilt aquarium. The April 2003 edition of the inflight Lufthansa Magazin printed a simulation of the Media City Port under the heading 'Hamburg's bold aspirations'. But the project, much-vaunted as a 'superlative landmark', remained an illusion. In October 2002, Ole von Beust spoke for the first time in public of a 'cultural and architectural highlight' for the Hafen-City, roughly estimating the anticipated costs at €50 million.

The third historic coincidence happened during a boat ride in October: Gérard was visited by Christine Binswanger. A senior partner at Herzog & de Meuron, she wanted to see Kaispeicher A up close. At a moment that could not have been better chosen had it been scripted, the autumn sky launched an attack of charm: sunlight streamed down, illuminating the aged and striking block of brick on the banks of the Elbe. Immediately, Christine Binswanger was reminded of the lagoon-bordered Venetian island of San Giorgio Maggiore.

While policymakers hesitated, the private project-developer Alexander Gérard pressed on undeterred. With the aim of

CULTURE AND CONGRESS CENTRE, LUCERNE

PHILHARMONIE, BERLIN

6 JUNE

26 JUNE

JUNE 2003

JULY 2003

First write-up in the Hamburger Abendblatt
of the construction plans for the port, entitled:
'Elbphilharmonie in Kaispeicher A?'

Herzog & de Meuron present their initial
designs in the basement of the Laeiszhalle.

PHILHARMONIE DE PARIS, PARIS

21 AUGUST

26 SEPTEMBER

AUGUST 2003　　　　　　　　　　　　SEPTEMBER 2003　　　　　　　　　　OCTOBER 2003

Several Hamburg architects write an
open letter to Ole von Beust championing
the 'great project'.

The SPD opposition urges the Senate to
abandon the Culture Senator's plans for
the AquaDome.

WALT DISNEY CONCERT HALL, LOS ANGELES

24 OCTOBER

NOVEMBER 2003

Official cessation of intent to build the Aqua-Dome, the long-time favourite for a major architectural project in the HafenCity.

5 DECEMBER

The Mayor and the Culture Senator announce that they intend to look over the plans for the Elbphilharmonie.

16 DECEMBER

DECEMBER 2003

The Bürgerschaft settles on Kaispeicher A as the location. The amount first forecasted by the city comes to between €91 and €93 million in construction costs.

winning over more advocates, he drafted a six-page pro-spectus that stated: 'The construction of a modern concert hall in Kaispeicher A through extensive use of its existing material can be realized at a much lower cost than an entirely new building. The city of Hamburg is here presented with the one-time chance, not only to erect a much-needed new concert hall, but to do so quickly'. Alexander Gérard then went on to clinch the argument once and for all:

In April 2003, Lufthansa Magazin prints a simulation of Media City Port. However, it was already clear at the time that nothing would come of these 'bold aspirations'.

'COMPARED TO OTHER CITIES ACROSS THE NATION AND THE WORLD, THE MUSICAL LIFE OF HAMBURG—WITH THE EXCEPTION OF THE STAATSOPER—IS PRETTY PROVINCIAL. JUST IMAGINE THE POTENTIAL THAT SYDNEY WOULD HAVE WASTED WITH RESPECT TO ITS IMAGE IF THE CITY HAD CHOSEN TO BUILD AN OFFICE BUILDING INSTEAD OF AN OPERA HOUSE!'

Gérard estimated about €95 million for construction costs. The portion of the new building that would cloak the concert hall, a commercial outer shell containing apartments and a hotel, was supposed to be a source of funding that would go towards those costs—meaning that building it would be practically free of charge to the city. 2005: start of construction.

29 FEBRUARY

JANUARY 2004   FEBRUARY 2004   MARCH 2004

The CDU wins an absolute majority in the parliamentary election. Soon after, Ole von Beust appoints Karin von Welck as Culture Senator.

26 MARCH

APRIL 2004

First email from Alexander Gérard to
the acoustician Yasuhisa Toyota.

17 MAY

MAY 2004

The Senate appoints Hartmut Wegener
as project coordinator.

Kaispeicher A in its original condition
with a historic harbour crane.

22/23 AUGUST

JUNE 2004   JULY 2004   AUGUST 2004

First meeting of the expert advisory
board of the Elbphilharmonie in the
guest house of the Senate.

2008: completion. Just in time for the centennial of the Laeiszhalle. Those were, so far, the plans.

In order to move the stalled debate forward, Gérard encouraged the architects to produce design elements that would help win over sceptics. Herzog & de Meuron are known for their attention to detail, for tinkering with a design until it is exactly right. A number of models and detailed designs emerged at this stage. Years later, a retrospective at the Haus der Kunst in Munich showed how the formal language of major Herzog & de Meuron projects—which at the time numbered 230—developed and changed over the course of time. Yet no matter how painstaking all of this close attention to detail might be, what was needed was a clear picture: something to turn heads, to catch eyes. After all, the opposition did not give the impression that it would consider altering its plans, at least not quickly and voluntarily. In June 2003, the Media City Port investors even obtained a preliminary building permit for their media offices, and for Jürgen Bruns-Berentelg, the head of HafenCity's development management, Gerard's Kaispeicher concept was 'at the moment, for economic and location-related reasons, not a good idea'.

The new Senate might have declared 'Wachsende Stadt' ('growing city') as its slogan and guiding intent, but it had not considered an investment in culture as a method of growing the city's prestige. However, after losing the national candidacy for the 2016 Summer Olympics in April (historical coincidence number four), policy turned to a search for a new line of action that would improve Hamburg's profile. 'Elbphilharmonie on Kaispeicher A?' That was the headline of an article appearing in the Hamburger Abendblatt in June. In it, the project was broadly described for the first time. This description included a large hall 'with a stage at its centre and seats for about 2,400', as well as a smaller one with a capacity for 500 visitors. The external commercial building, complemented by funding from an association, a foundation or sponsors, would reportedly finance the reconstruction and the majority of the operating costs. Rolf Beck, at the time both director of the NDR Orchester and artistic director of the Schleswig-Holstein Musik Festival, reacted with great pleasure: 'The idea of the AquaDome is like the proverbial pair of birds in the bush. But the Kaispeicher concept contains everything that Hamburg needs. All that remains is to convince the Senator of Culture to drop her AquaDome.'

Benedikt Stampa, managing director of the Laeiszhalle, summed up the opportunities offered by the concept as follows: 'New rooms give rise to new contents.' When Alexander Gérard brought a model made of wood and plastic to the Office of Monument Protection, its head was also enthusiastic.

Gérard and Marko presented their concept on 26 June 2003 at a press conference in the Laeiszhalle Studio E. 'Urban development needs visionaries, but in order to do more than imagine a project such as this one, a majority of the city must stand behind it,' said Pierre de Meuron, and Alexander Gérard reiterated that the sale of apartments would regulate project finances. The additional funding necessary, amounting to between €25 and €30 million, would come—hopefully—from donors. The city would need to make the land available free of charge for development and use. Only the actual operating costs of concerts were not included in Gérard's calculations.

An open letter, addressed to the First Mayor and signed by a dozen well-known Hamburg architects, provided further impetus to the project. On 21 August, a letter of recommendation was sent by the architects' Swiss colleagues to Ole von Beust: 'Hamburg has the once-in-a-lifetime chance to prove itself, and emphatically claim the global status it has so long sought. The concept is inspired. It is a must for the city.' The shift in public and political opinion had begun. Alexander Gérard's plan was officially approved, and shortly afterwards Mayor von Beust, now convinced, declared: 'The city needs a landmark for the 21st century: one with influence that

7 SEPT. 10 SEPTEMBER

3 NOVEMBER

SEPTEMBER 2004

OCTOBER 2004

The Senate commissions ReGe to conduct a feasibility study.

The Senate concludes an agreement with the investors Alexander Gérard and Dieter Becken towards the realization of the Elbphilharmonie.

The city buys Alexander Gérard and Dieter Becken out of their contract.

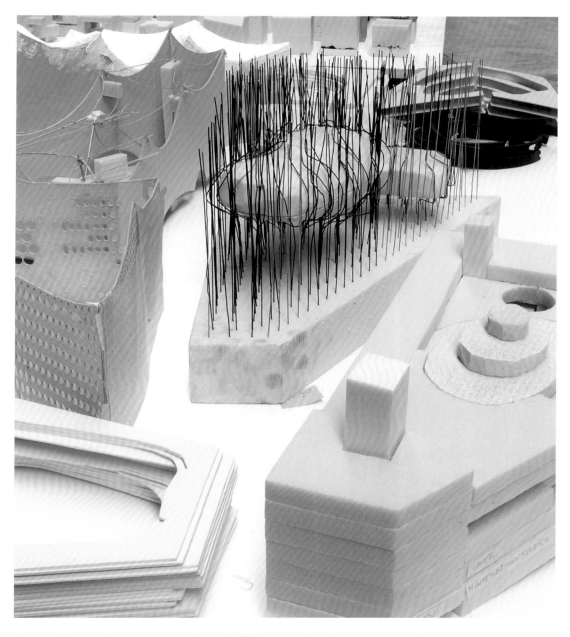

At an exhibition at Munich's Haus der Kunst in 2006, Herzog & de Meuron present individual steps leading to the final form of the Elbphilharmonie.

12 JANUARY   **19 JANUARY**

NOVEMBER 2004   DECEMBER 2004   JANUARY 2005

Return to the historical name: Signing of the General
the Musikhalle is renamed the   Planner Contract between
Laeiszhalle.   the architects and the city.

In February 2006, a banner announces the Elbphilharmonie.
A model on the roof of Kaispeicher A provides a taste of the
building to come.

radiates beyond our national borders. A Philharmonie built
atop Kaispeicher A could be just the ticket'.

City Hall had finally recognized that the concept of HafenCity
as a symbol of the 'growing city' would require a distinguished
architectural address that would turn heads, a reliable source
of striking images, a magnet that could draw crowds; but also
an incentive for investors, for whom an attractive jewel in the
neighbourhood would make doing business more pleasant.
On 16 December 2003, the Senate therefore decided to pursue
the Elbphilharmonie project on the site of Kaispeicher A. The
accompanying opinion stated, clearly and eloquently, that
'every subsequent design for a new concert hall taking up a
less prominent place in the city's landscape will be measured
against the concept of the Elbphilharmonie'.

One of several price forecasts now predicted construction
costs ranging from €91 to €96 million. But there were also
experts who calculated an estimated €146 million in capital
expenditure. From the outset, it was clear that Herzog & de
Meuron's design would need to be taken as a whole or not at
all—much like a painting done by a famous master over which
one was no longer allowed to paint. And yet there was no
serious talk of putting the Elbphilharmonie out to tender, a
move that would normally be expected for an urban project of
this size. Two weeks later, the Bürgerschaft ruled that new
elections would be held. For some time, City Hall had more
important matters on its mind. After it was all over, the course
was set anew. As a member of the CDU, Mayor von Beust could
now govern backed by an absolute majority. He separated
from his former Senator of Culture, brought Karin von Welck
from Berlin to take up the office, and appointed as the project
coordinator Hartmut Wegener, head of ReGe, the city-owned
construction management company responsible for coordin-
ating building projects in the city. The Japanese acoustician
Yasuhisa Toyota was contracted as the project's acoustician.
In actuality, this came as no surprise, because his company,

24 FEBRUARY

FEBRUARY 2005   MARCH 2005

The Elbphilharmonie is put out to tender
in a Europe-wide invitation to bid.

Nagata Acoustics, had already built up a large international reputation for success when it came to the harmonious marriage of architectural ideas to physical realities.

Planning had begun in Basel on the banks of the Rhine; now, on the banks of the Elbe, a panel of experts, assembled from an international roster of concert-house managers, was called together to make recommendations for local cultural policy. The legendary Ernest Fleischmann was flown in from Los Angeles. He was credited with pulling the strings to make the Frank Gehry-designed Walt Disney Concert Hall a reality. From New York came Klaus Jacobs, vice chairman and chief financial officer of Carnegie Hall. From Amsterdam came Martijn Sanders, director of the Concertgebouw. These were, without exception, professionals who knew which things had to be pushed through and which things were better left untouched. Also on the agenda was the essential question of who would be capable of taking on the role—as seductive as it was risky—of 'founding artistic director' of the Elbphilharmonie. In November 2004, Alexander Gérard no longer wanted to continue. He and his business partner Dieter Becken accepted a buyout of €3 million from the city and left the project. This separation, which necessitated that they relinquish all of their rights, was a painful blow for Gérard and Marko. According to the accompanying press release, the two project developers 'saw their mission as successfully completed'.

The next noteworthy date was 19 January 2005: this day marked the signing in ReGe's offices of the 'General Planner Contract', which was supposed to govern all open questions between the city and the architects. But in the years to come, this turned out to have been plain wishful thinking, because responsibility for the so-called 'detailed design' in structurally relevant areas remained that of Herzog & de Meuron, even after the awarding of the contract to the building company. The fact that the architects were under contract to the city and not the future building company ensured from the start that there would be conflicts with the developer. After all, Hochtief had already guaranteed the city a fixed total cost for the project without knowledge of the final plans. Even at this very early stage, the Elbphilharmonie was worlds away from being an ordinary construction site. Nearly all of the elements involved would be tricky. Most components would have to be custom-fabricated, thus making everything ultra-challenging. And ultra-expensive. When the Elbphilharmonie was put out to tender in a Europe-wide invitation to bid, architect Jacques Herzog said:

'THE PHILHARMONIE IS AN ICON. I ONLY TRUST THAT THE LEADERSHIP OF HAMBURG UNDERSTANDS THAT.'

It had reached the point where every angle of the concept could be, should be, and indeed had to be planned out, and with speed. For this reason, a major public hearing was staged in August 2005. In the City Hall banquet room, 60 representatives had gathered, comprising members of the committees on budget, culture and urban development issues. Fourteen experts would be there to answer questions over the course of two long evenings. One of them was Volkwin Marg, an internationally successful Hamburg architect with many major buildings under his belt. 'If you're going to make a decision of such epic proportions, you have to show your colours. No cathedral of the mind was ever built according to narrow-minded standards.' However, Marg also issued a warning against the dangers of politically motivated and therefore ultimately theoretical cost estimates that were overly optimistic. The intellectual stature of the hearing was a first

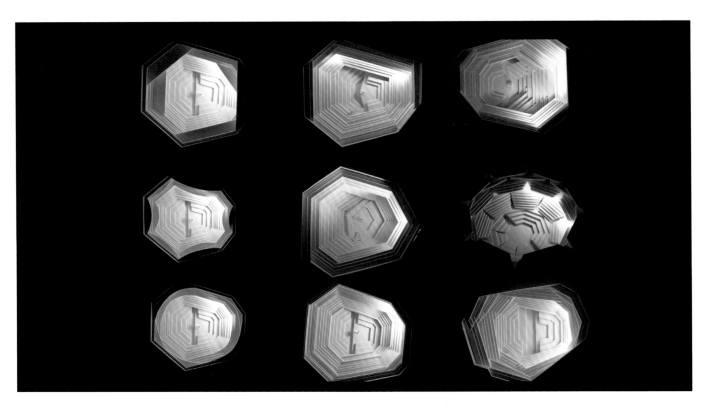

Above: in the early phase of planning, the architects and the acoustician experiment over and over with possible forms for the hall to take. Bottom left: diagram of the sound reflector, which had not yet been foreseen in the initial design of the Grand Hall (right).

23 24 AUGUST

JULY 2005

The city's feasibility study assumes €187.7 million in construction costs and predicts that the city's portion will be €77 million.

AUGUST 2005

Fourteen experts from around the world deliver speeches—and answers—to the Bürgerschaft in City Hall.

Hannelore and Helmut Greve, business leaders, donate €30 million for construction costs.

indication of the many debates that were to follow in the coming years, addressing the pros and cons, the hows and, above all, the how muches of each element of the project.

The Austrian Christoph Lieben-Seutter, still artistic director of the Wiener Konzerthaus at the time, was also among the foreign guests. As an observer, he commented with humour on the guts it took the people of Hamburg to be so staunchly unique: 'Consider yourselves lucky that there's no readymade shoebox-style concert hall available straight off the racks.'

A few weeks later, a second consultation round, this time in the Hamburg Chamber of Crafts, addressed the sponsorship concept, financing and economics. The first official announcement, a feasibility study immortalized in a 125-page printed document issued by the Bürgerschaft, set the cost at €186.7 million. Line items were: €94.7 million for the Elbphilharmonie itself, €69.6 million for the development of the commercial 'cladding' (hotel, apartments, car park, eateries), as well as €22.4 million for 'special infrastructural costs', including the Plaza, which would act as a junction between the old warehouse and the new structure above it.

To limit the city's share of the costs, the city had set itself the ambitious goal of generating up to €30 million in donations. This would mean that, after deduction of donations and cross-subsidies, its costs would come to €77 million, at most. 'If everything goes wrong, the price will be €77 million,' said the mayor, and this was a 'pessimistic guess'.

'THE ELBPHILHARMONIE IS DOABLE, IF WE WANT TO DO IT.'

In August the matter continued to gain momentum. This was ensured by three cheques written by private donors as advance payments in an attempt to get the ball rolling. Helmut and Hannelore Greve made a start with €30 million. These two patrons had given the city a similar gift in the 1990s to support the construction of two wings of the university. Approximately one month after their bequest to the Elbphilharmonie, First Mayor Ole von Beust declared the Greves 'citizens of honour'. Shortly after, the businessman Michael Otto and the Hermann Reemtsma Foundation each added €10 million to the pile. Thus, the goal set for 'affordable contributions' was exceeded, just a few weeks after it was proclaimed as only being achievable in the medium term.

The Elbphilharmonie Foundation began the search for sponsors and patrons at the end of October 2005. It was at least equally important to lay the psychological groundwork in the city. It was felt that the wave of enthusiasm must not subside. Major donors such as the Greves were of course welcome, but the enthusiasm of medium and small donors was indispensable in order to anchor the cultural idea behind the spectacular facade. A 'house for everyone' would have to be supported by more than just a few.

Another important sign: the Körber Foundation, with offices located just a block away from the Elbphilharmonie, gave €3 million as starting capital to establish a 'Fund for the Future of Music' that would promote youth and music-education programmes. It signalled that the project was no longer just a clever mind game, but a reality, and a historic opportunity to boot. And during a session of the Bürgerschaft, the former Senator of Urban Development Willfried Mayer said: 'Something surprising has come to pass: Hamburg, the city of businesspeople, is making a new symbol for itself. It is erecting a temple to the muses, which will for the first time be allowed to intervene once again in the Hamburg skyline and to round out the assembly of church towers. This is a sign that the city is ready to surpass its own prospects.'

The next giant leap forward occurred in early December with the signing of a letter of intent. For €800,000 a year the NDR Sinfonieorchester was to be the Elbphilharmonie's

28 SEPTEMBER

SEPTEMBER 2005   OCTOBER 2005

Businessman Michael Otto donates
€10 million.

31 OCTOBER

NOVEMBER 2005

The Elbphilharmonie Foundation collects money in order to relieve the costs of construction for the city and to support the operation of the concert hall.

orchestra-in-residence: a ten-year term, starting with the Philharmonie's opening, which at that time people still believed would take place in four years.

During the long phase of planning and debates, the design of the new concert house had been taken as being final. However, in April 2006, the architects submitted a design update that showed significant changes. If the first version of the Grand Hall had been very round, version 2.0 had a more angular feel. Hitherto gently flowing balconies were replaced by vigorously interpenetrating levels. The colours had changed. There were now fewer seats behind the orchestra podium. Most importantly, there was a new element in the construction of the ceiling—a huge reflector above the stage.

The plan also included a new third hall for rehearsals and experimental performances with approximately 170 seats. A curved escalator had been added as well. Along with all of this came the modified glass facade. The uniformity of the surface had been artistically broken up. Particular panels would include openings made of curved glass that would provide optical variety, embedded in frames with shapes reminiscent of tuning forks. The architects had also decided to pattern the glass with dots. On the roof there would be two observation decks, offering singular panoramic views of the city and port.

In early June 2006, there was an official reunion at City Hall with one of the participants from the previous year's panel of experts: Christoph Lieben-Seutter of Vienna had made a good impression on the Department of Culture with his first visit. At the end of the search for an artistic director, he was hired as general artistic director of the Elbphilharmonie and Laeiszhalle. A father of three daughters, Lieben-Seutter was ready to leave Vienna—a city without equal in richness of musical tradition—for the port city of Hamburg and, as an aide to its cultural development, open a concert hall the like of which had never before existed. And this even after having delivered the sober diagnosis that 'Hamburg is no musical town' during his first visit to the Elbe and thereby having prophesied how much work lay before all involved. He wanted to open this concert house that still had neither a final price tag nor a settled design and plan. There were probably simpler jobs to be had out there in the big, colourful world of concert halls. In any case, one thing was guaranteed: no post came with more challenges. Initially, Lieben-Seutter's inauguration was set for the beginning of the 2007 season. Ultimately, almost another full decade would pass before the inaugural concert in the Grand Hall of the Elbphilharmonie. With the aim of countering sceptics and continuing to fuel anticipation, the Elbphilharmonie Foundation went public with a solidarity campaign: 'Hamburg is building a landmark'.

In August 2006, rumours began to circulate that the building costs had increased by some €34 million to €220 million. The parties responsible denied these rumours, asking the public for patience until the conclusion of the Europe-wide call for bids on 29 November. However, the construction costs were to rise still further and reach the €241.3 million mark. In addition, the city revealed a number of line items for the first time. The portion to be paid by the city increased from €77 to €114.3 million. The public were unaware that the city would now be the owner of the hotel, restaurant and parking garage, as well. Ole von Beust, Hamburg's mayor at the time, took it calmly:

'OUTSTANDING CULTURE AND ARCHITECTURE HAVE THEIR PRICE.'

The contract for the construction project was finally awarded to an investor consortium comprising Hochtief and Commerz-Leasing. Delays in construction would incur a contractual penalty of €200,000 per day.

29 NOVEMBER   **8 DECEMBER**

DECEMBER 2005

19 JANUARY

JANUARY 2006

The Hermann Reemtsma Foundation donates €10 million.

Contract signing in City Hall: the NDR Sinfonieorchester becomes the resident orchestra of the Elbphilharmonie.

The Körber Foundation gives €3 million to the artistic programme.

The good news: the Elbphilharmonie's first season would begin in May 2010. On 19 December 2006 the Senate gave the issue the green light; on 28 February the Bürgerschaft also approved it, unanimously, without the usual partisan discord. At noon on 2 April inside the Kaispeicher, a new era began. Hamburg had served its time without its Elbphilharmonie—now, the age of Hamburg with the Elbphilharmonie was beginning, and should be celebrated. A brass band from the NDR Sinfonieorchester and the members of the Philharmonie played Georg Friedrich Handel's 'Music for the Royal Fireworks', and First Mayor Ole von Beust announced: 'We're not bluffing—it's really happening.' The event was officially declared a ground-breaking ceremony. This was only partially true; after all, ground had been broken long ago for the historic Kaispeicher A, which serves as the foundation of the building complex.

And yet, even without the laying of a proper foundation stone, the approximately 700 invited guests were still rewarded with a great deal of pleasant symbolism. There were major speeches and, as the climax of the day, a copper time capsule was filled and given a place of honour in the surrogate foundation stone. There it rests, containing a certificate, a golden coin specially embossed by the Hamburger Münzanstalt (Hamburg Mint) and bearing an image of the Elbphilharmonie, a stylus commemorating the donors, euro coins minted in Hamburg, newspapers of the day, informational material about the city in general and about the building in particular, and various architectural drawings. A brick was stamped during the ceremony in honour of each participant. And Pierre de Meuron named the Elbphilharmonie the 'new centre of social, cultural and public life' in Hamburg.

On 2 April 2007, the visionary dream of Alexander Gérard and Jana Marko had become reality—almost.

First major donors, then citizens of honour: Hamburg patrons Hannelore and Helmut Greve (†). On the 13th floor of the Elbphilharmonie, a foyer is named the 'Helmut and Hannelore Greve Foyer'.

18 APRIL

FEBRUARY 2006   MARCH 2006   APRIL 2006

Architects submit   Construction costs
a design update.   rise again, this time
    to €228.6 million.

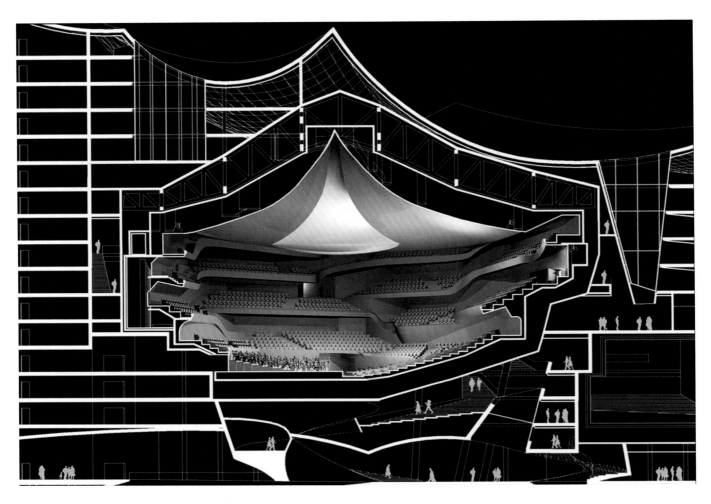

Cross-section of the Grand Hall. Clearly visible:
the sound reflector above the stage.

6 JUNE

27 JUNE

MAY 2006   JUNE 2006   JULY 2006

Christoph Lieben-Seutter, head of the Wiener Konzerthaus,
is presented at City Hall as the general artistic director of
the Elbphilharmonie and the Laeiszhalle.

The Department of Culture submits a
request for a third performance stage
in the Elbphilharmonie.

OLE VON BEUST
FIRST MAYOR OF THE FREE HANSEATIC
CITY OF HAMBURG

The lawyer and Christian Democratic Union (CDU) politician became the First Mayor of Hamburg in 2001. The idea for the Elbphilharmonie was born during his term. Von Beust recognized in the plan for the new concert hall a cultural site that would be the source of great charisma and international renown, and saw its construction as a historical opportunity for the city. Ole von Beust made important moves to set the course, but he was also incumbent in City Hall when costs exploded and timelines fell apart. These were problems that another mayor would have to solve—in the summer of 2010, Ole von Beust handed in his resignation.

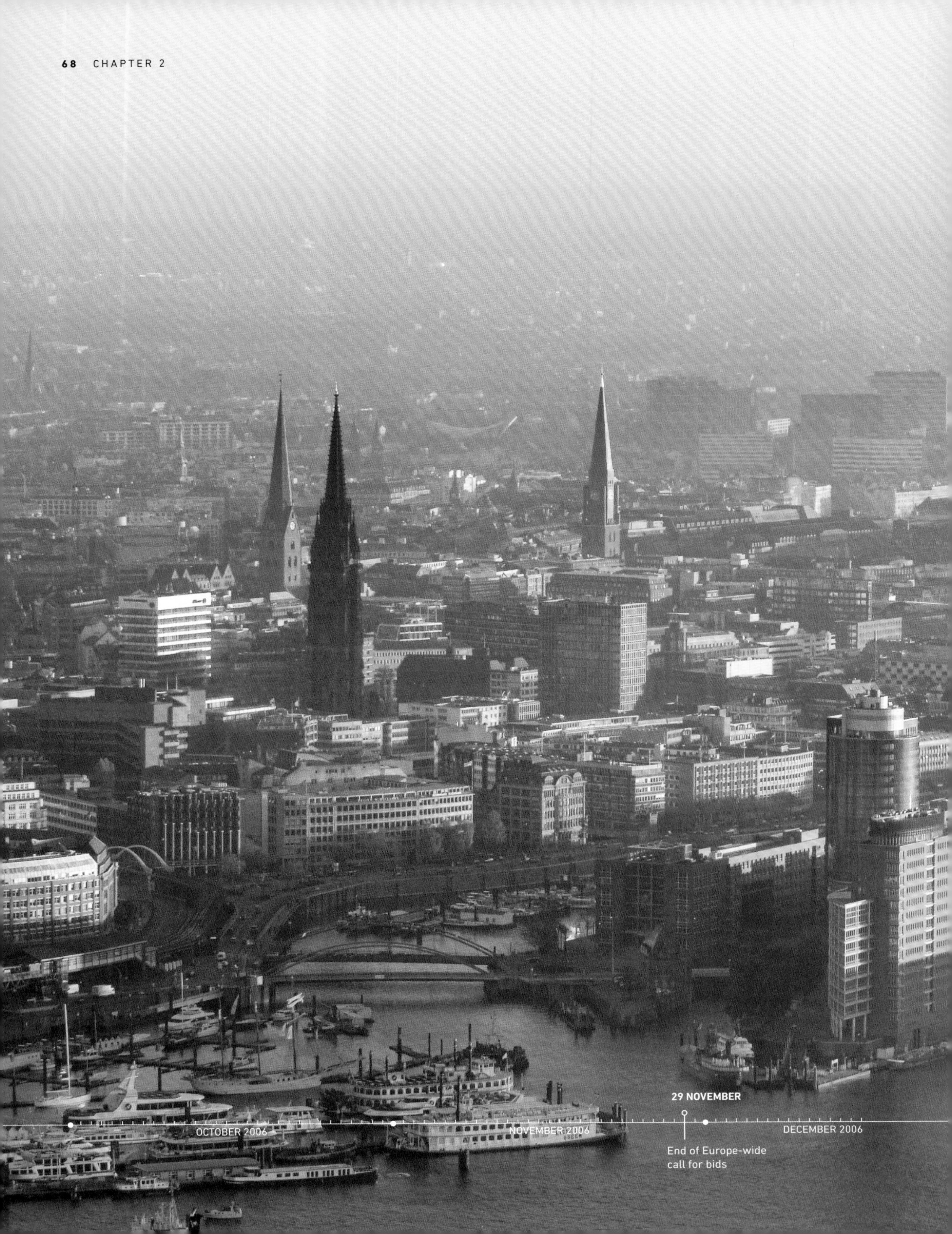
OCTOBER 2006
NOVEMBER 2006
29 NOVEMBER
End of Europe-wide call for bids
DECEMBER 2006

Large sections of the HafenCity remain undeveloped in 2005. Kaispeicher A stands sadly at the tip; behind it, many open spaces lie fallow.

18/19 DECEMBER

JANUARY 2007

Ole von Beust announces the result of the call for bids. The Elbphilharmonie will be more elaborate, and more expensive, than planned. Construction costs rise to €241.3 million. The city's portion now amounts to €114.3 million (instead of €77 million).

1 FEBRUARY

FEBRUARY 2007

Founding of the Elbphilharmonie Bau KG, which acts as the builder-owner.

Kaispeicher A is completely gutted by the end of 2007. To strengthen the foundation, 650 additional reinforced-concrete piles are driven into the earth.

30 MARCH

28 MARCH   2 APRIL

MARCH 2007   APRIL 2007   MAY 2007

A Hamburg delegation   Contract amendment 1:   Symbolic laying of foundation stone,
presents the project at   Herzog & de Meuron says   construction begins. Supposedly, everything
Carnegie Hall, New York.   the planned schedule is   will be completed within three years.
                             too tight.

Construction Site

Here, a state of emergency is normality.
Strong nerves and a lot of patience are needed.

Complications, conflicts, skyrocketing costs.

Impressions of a Gesamtkunstwerk made of
concrete, glass, steel, and mighty dreams.

4 AUGUST

AUGUST 2007

A 300-ton crane heaves five excavators onto the roof of the Kaispeicher. They work their way down through the building, one storey at a time.

26 SEPTEMBER

SEPTEMBER 2007

OCTOBER 2007

Businessman Peter Möhrle donates around €2 million for the building of the concert organ.

Dance of the cranes, February 2008: HafenCity, Hamburg's new riverside district, is Europe's largest urban development project, with the Elbphilharmonie as the crown jewel of the development.

7 NOVEMBER

NOVEMBER 2007

DECEMBER 2007

23 October, contract amendment 2 concerning €0.5 million in extra interest payments.

Celebrities auction their favourite items of clothing to raise money for the Elbphilharmonie Foundation.

Above: by early 2009, Kaispeicher A's brick facade is completely surrounded with scaffolding. In order not to further raise the weight of the building—estimated at 200,000 tons—interstices in the steel reinforcements are filled with hollow artificial fibre.
Right: the Grand Hall is put together piece by piece, like a puzzle, October 2009.

30 JANUARY

25 FEBRUARY

JANUARY 2008   FEBRUARY 2008   MARCH 2008

A wrecking permit is
issued for the building.

The competition to build the organ
is won by the Klais workshop, a
Bonn-based family business.

2 APRIL

APRIL 2008   MAY 2008

In the Hamburg parliament, Culture
Senator Karin von Welck denies reports
that the project's costs are exploding.

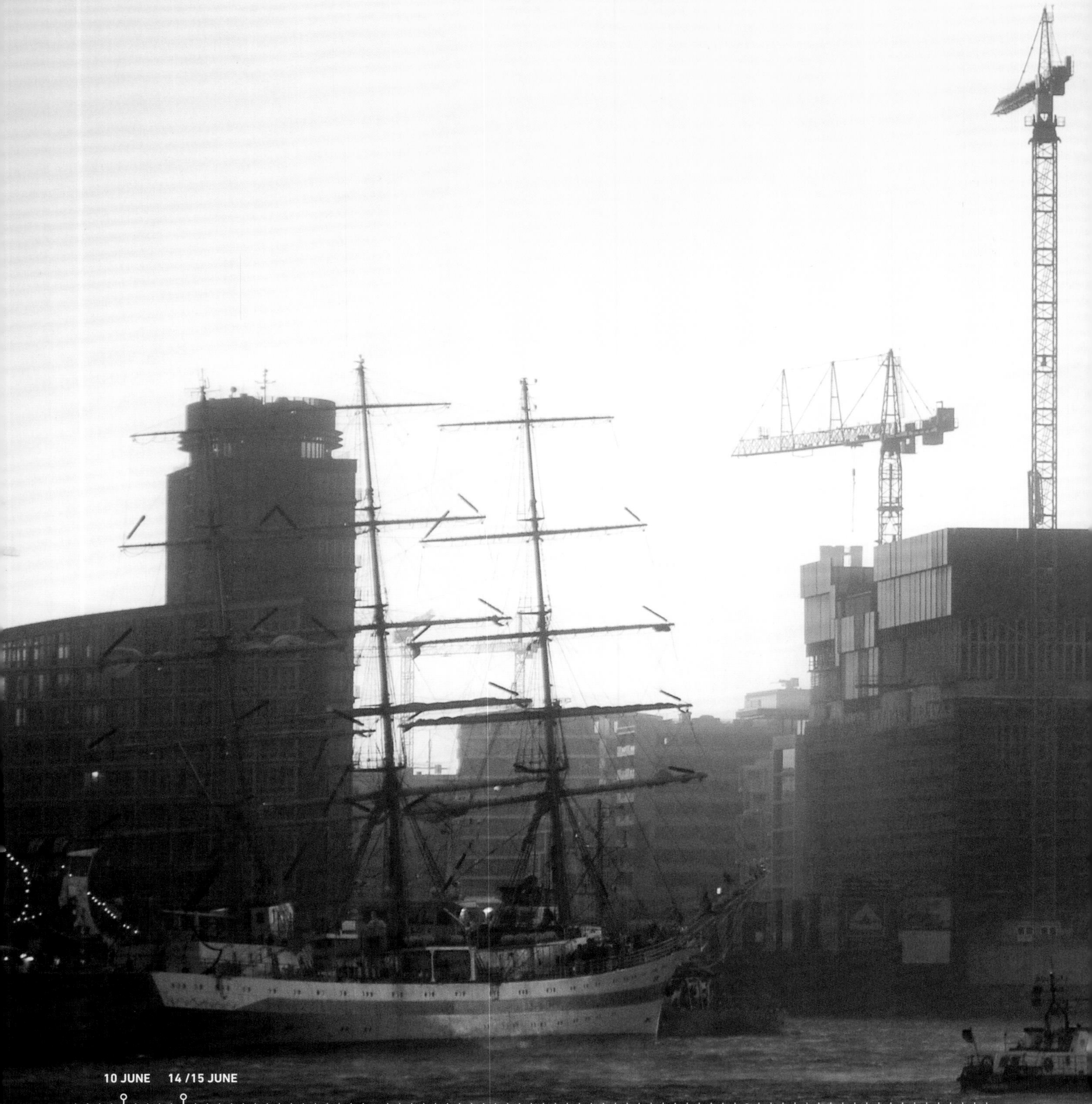

10 JUNE 14 /15 JUNE

JUNE 2008 JULY 2008 AUGUST 2008

May 2009 sees a storm
sweep over Hamburg,
violently shaking the cranes.
It threatens to submerge
Hamburg's 820th 'Port
Anniversary'.

2 OCTOBER

SEPTEMBER 2008

OCTOBER 2008

Opening of the Elbphilharmonie
Pavilion on the Magellan-Terrassen.

18,000 tons of steel and 63,000 cubic
metres of concrete are used during
the course of the construction, 2009.

13 DECEMBER

26 November, contract amendment 4:
taxpayer costs rise from €114.3 to a putative
€495 million. Planned opening: early 2012.

Construction work reaches the
Plaza level on the 8th floor.

Beginning of work on the new
building on top of the Kaispeicher.
Waves of glass begin to grow.

APRIL 2009

MAY 2009

3 JUNE

JUNE 2009

Work begins on the shell in the
concert area of the building.

The so-called 'inner bowl' of the 'pot'—the Grand Hall—has hardly a single flat surface. Balconies, ledges, steel ribs and staircases are mounted before the building is complete, then lifted by crane, through the still-open roof, March 2010.

25 JUNE

JULY 2009

AUGUST 2009

The first of four cranes is increased in height from 82 to 111 metres.

SEPTEMBER 2009   OCTOBER 2009   NOVEMBER 2009

The cocoon for the acoustically-isolated Grand Hall is ready. In March 2010, the outer shell, made of reinforced concrete, is attached to the remainder of the building.

16 DECEMBER

DECEMBER 2009

Mounting of the glass facade begins: The first elements are installed around 40 metres above ground level.

JANUARY 2010

12 January: Hochtief announces that the Elbphilharmonie will be completed by the end of 2012, refers to €22.4 million in additional costs.

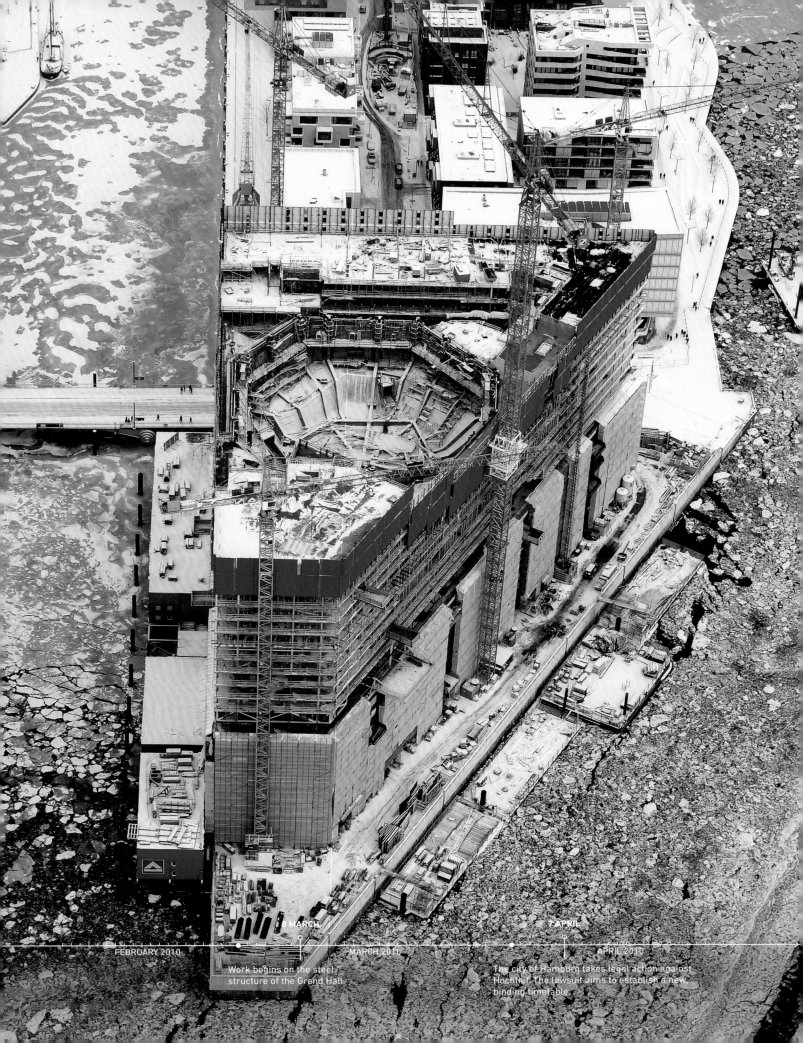

8 MARCH

7 APRIL

MARCH 2010

APRIL 2010

Work begins on the steel
structure of the Grand Hall.

The city of Hamburg takes legal action against
Hochtief. The lawsuit aims to establish a new,
binding timetable.

Drifting ice on the Elbe and snow in the Grand Hall make construction much more difficult in the winter of 2010. Seen from above, the building looks like a hollow tooth.

5 MAY

28 MAY

26 JUNE

MAY 2010

JUNE 2010

The Bürgerschaft, or parliament, establishes a first parliamentary commission of inquiry.

Topping-out ceremony, more than three years after the foundation stone was laid. While celebrations take place on the Plaza, protest demonstrations are held in front of the building.

Work begins on the steel structure of the building's roof.

18 JULY

25 AUGUST

JULY 2010

AUGUST 2010

SEPTEMBER 2010

First Mayor Ole von Beust announces his resignation. The Culture Senator also resigns.

Christoph Ahlhaus (CDU) is voted into office as the city's new mayor, Reinhard Stuth is named Culture Senator.

In April 2010, new meets old. It has been a long time since new ships have been constructed in the Blohm+Voss floating dock, but around ten cruise ships a year are serviced here.

7 NOVEMBER

OCTOBER 2010   NOVEMBER 2010

Completion of steel balconies in the Grand Hall.

28 NOVEMBER

End of the Christian Democrat-Green Party coalition.

20 FEBRUARY

Elections to the city parliament, with the
Social Democrats winning an absolute
majority. Olaf Scholz becomes First Mayor.

Art under construction: the parking garage's spiral shaft, with room for 521 cars, winds impressively upwards. On the Plaza, 37 metres up, around 1,400 guests celebrate the topping-out ceremony.

17 MARCH

23 MARCH

19 APRIL

MARCH 2011

APRIL 2011

MAY 2011

Hochtief presents a new timetable: final completion will take place in ten months—at the end of November 2013.

New Culture Senator Barbara Kisseler takes office.

A second parliamentary commission of inquiry into the Elbphilharmonie begins work.

The Grand Hall awaits
completion, May 2010.

15 JUNE

20 SEPTEMBER

30 SEPTEMBER

AUGUST 2011   SEPTEMBER 2011   OCTOBER 2011

Doubts are raised concerning the building's statics. For safety
reasons, Hochtief suspends work on the hall roof.

Hochtief suspends further
planning work.

When completed, the 'wave'
above the Kaispeicher will weigh
78,000 tons, with a facade of
16,000 square metres, May 2011.

7 FEBRUARY

21 FEBRUARY

JANUARY 2012   FEBRUARY 2012   MARCH 2012

Construction supervisors confirm they have no reservations   Hochtief withdraws a third of its
regarding the safety of the roof. Hamburg's project   workforce from the site.
management company demands Hochtief continues
construction.

11 APRIL

Looking out from the
western summit of the
Elbphilharmonie, with a
view over HafenCity, the
Speicherstadt (a UNESCO
World Heritage Site) and
Hamburg's Altstadt,
January 2012.

21 JUNE

5 JULY

JUNE 2012

JULY 2012

AUGUST 2012

A further ultimatum is presented to Hochtief,
demanding that the building company presents a
binding declaration on remaining work by 28 June.

The city and Hochtief come to an agreement:
the roof will be installed, and the building is
to be completed by mid-2015.

The view of one of the world's best concert halls reconciles the people of Hamburg to the project. Despite the skyrocketing costs, according to an August 2011 survey, 70 per cent of the city's inhabitants are enthusiastic to see it brought to completion.

27 AUGUST

29 SEPTEMBER

AUGUST 2012   SEPTEMBER 2012   OCTOBER 2012

Culture Senator Kisseler and Marcelino Fernández
Verdes of Hochtief meet in Venice for a crisis summit.

First public concert on the Plaza: a staged
version of Brahms's German Requiem.

Hochtief declares installation of the roof complete, without complications.

From 15 December, one contract governs relations between the developers and the construction firm. But construction costs rise to €575 million.

Resignation of Heribert Leutner, head of ReGe, the city project management agency.

15 FEBRUARY

FEBRUARY 2013

Former mayor Ole von Beust is
the final witness called before the
parliamentary commission of inquiry.

MARCH 2013

Almost at the summit: the last touches are put on the peak of the building's roof. Left: even the stairs to the Grand Hall are taking shape, January 2012.

9 APRIL

APRIL 2013   MAY 2013   JUNE 2013

19 JUNE

Completion of project reorganization; signing of new contract.

23 April: contract amendment 5 accepted. Total price, including all ancillary costs: €865 million. Cost to city of Hamburg: €789 million.

Hamburg parliament gives the green light to the restructured contract. Construction work can restart.

At its highest point, the roof of the Elbphilharmonie is 110 metres high, only 22 metres lower than the tower of St. Michaelis. The concert hall offers many spectacular views. To build it, 1,100 glass elements were manufactured in Italy, then all bent into individual shapes and printed with patterns. The roof is constructed to withstand hurricane-force gusts and rain on a Biblical scale.

3 JULY

JULY 2013   AUGUST 2013

First joint public appearance of representatives
of the city, architects and building company since
the topping-out ceremony.

4 NOVEMBER

13 DECEMBER

DECEMBER 2013

The first of approximately 10,000 gypsum
fibre panels making up the 'white skin' are
installed in the Grand Hall.

31 JANUARY

JANUARY 2014

At 1.21 pm, in icy temperatures, the last glass
element is mounted on the building's facade.

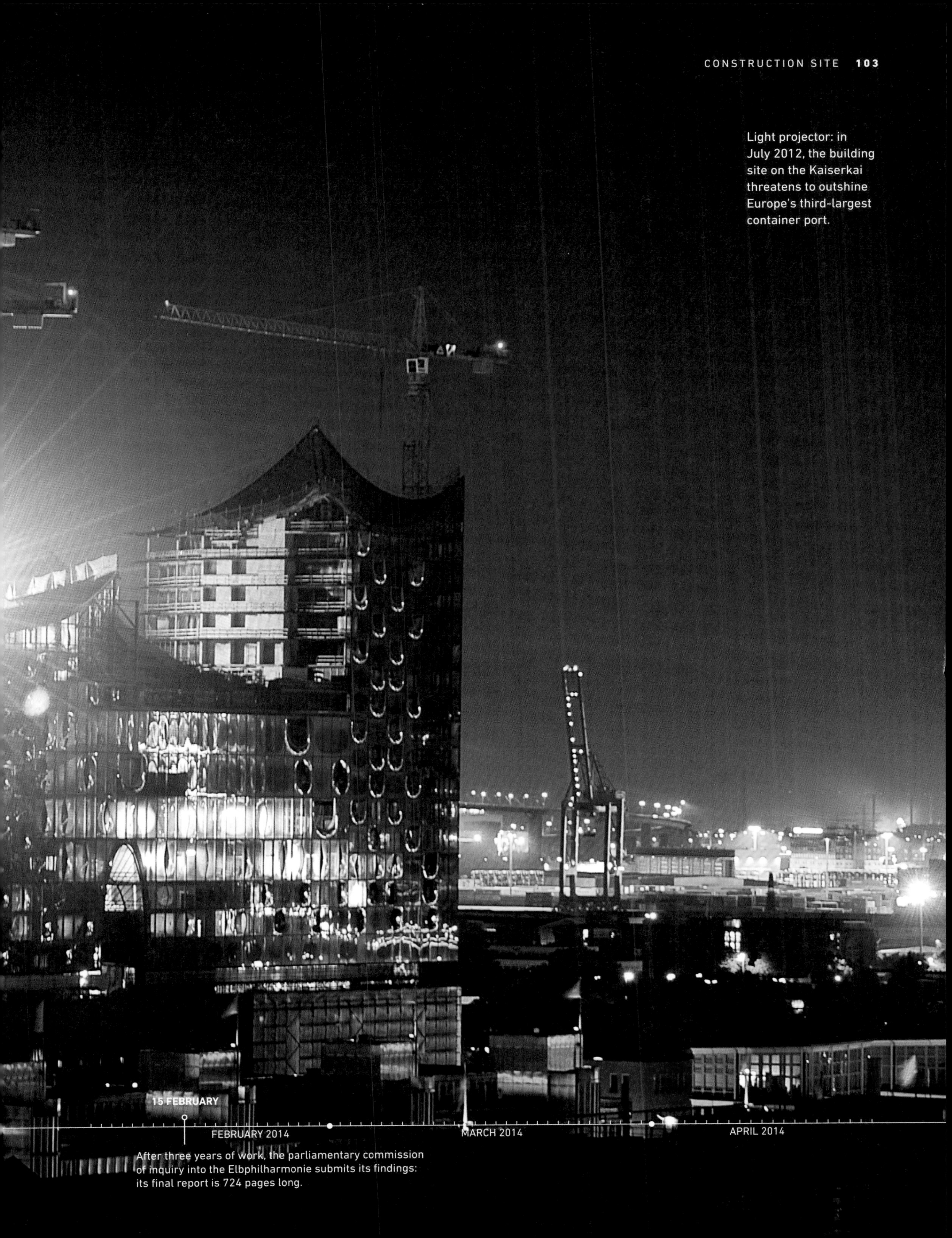

Light projector: in July 2012, the building site on the Kaiserkai threatens to outshine Europe's third-largest container port.

15 FEBRUARY

FEBRUARY 2014 | MARCH 2014 | APRIL 2014

After three years of work, the parliamentary commission of inquiry into the Elbphilharmonie submits its findings: its final report is 724 pages long.

7 MAY

MAY 2014

JUNE 2014

The Bürgerschaft, or Hamburg
parliament, signs off on the final report
of the parliamentary commission.

Left: the Queen Mary 2 has room for 2,620 passengers. Precisely the right number to fill both of the Elbphilharmonie's concert halls. In August 2013, the seagoing queen and the new queen of concert halls finally meet. Above: the stairway leading from the Plaza to the Recital Hall, spectacular view included.

15 AUGUST

JULY 2014   AUGUST 2014   SEPTEMBER 2014

The roof, with its 6,000 giant sequins, is completed exactly on time. Interior construction can now be continued regardless of weather conditions.

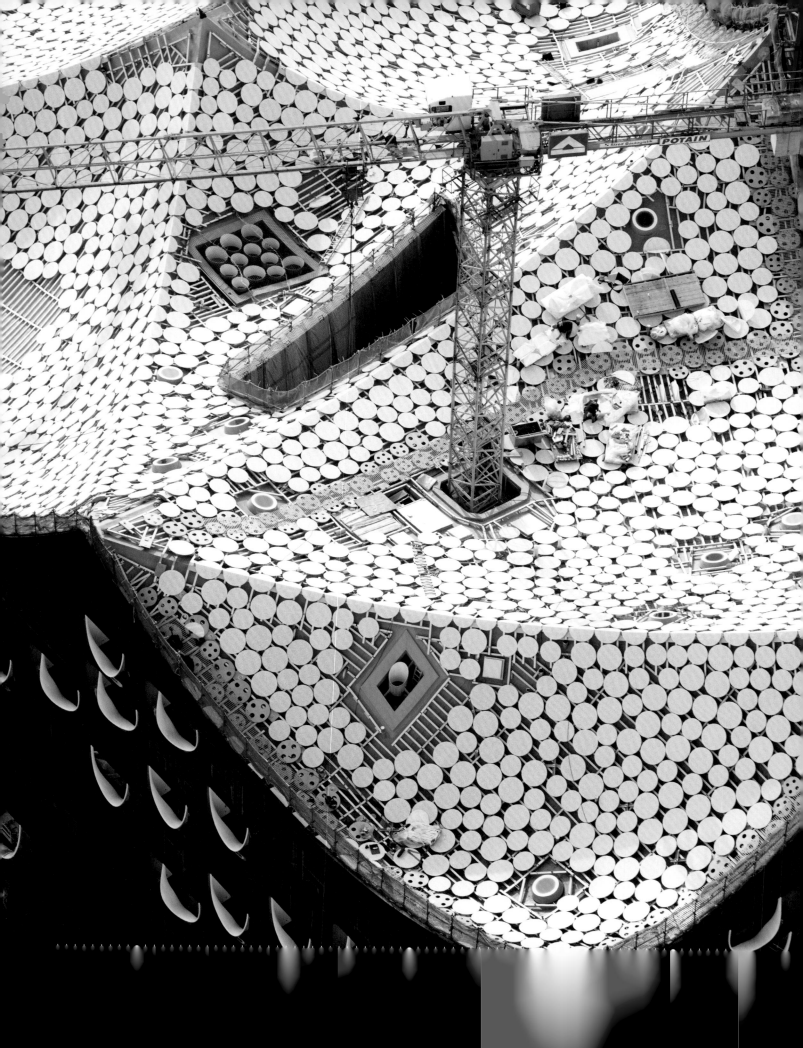

Left: in April 2015, the roof's wave surfaces are filling up: 6,000 giant sequins sparkle like dancing waves.
Above: invisible to visitors is the elaborate fire-prevention technology behind the scenes.
Below: the facade of the Elbphilharmonie towers above neighbouring buildings.

24 DECEMBER   **12 JANUARY 2015**

DECEMBER 2014   JANUARY 2015   FEBRUARY 2015

Building work on the Tube
is completed.

At the construction site of the Grand Hall, Mayor
Olaf Scholz announces the official opening date of
the Elbphilharmonie: 11 January 2017.

76 X 75 X660
72 X N

CE

Say hello, Christo!
Until the construction
project is completed,
the Recital Hall's
ceiling lamps are
wrapped to protect
them against damage
and dirt, July 2015.

30 APRIL

MARCH 2015   APRIL 2015

The Grand Hall is completed on time.
Technology for ventilation and smoke
extraction is installed. It weighs 8,000 tons.

17 MAY

MAY 2015

Maiden voyage of the river boat
MS Elbphilharmonie, which hosts
information events.

26 JUNE

JUNE 2015

Public presentation of construction
progress on the Plaza. Culture Senator
Kisseler: 'I'm flabbergasted!'

14 JULY

JULY 2015

Complete dismantling of last
construction crane.

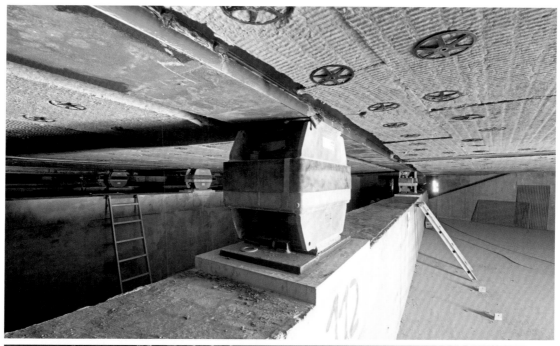

A glimpse behind the scenes: the Grand Hall resting on steel-spring elements, which isolate it acoustically from the rest of the building. Red is a warning: 'Do not drill here!' On a site visit in January 2015, Hamburg's First Mayor Olaf Scholz announces the date of the opening concert, pausing slightly before naming the year.

21 NOVEMBER

OCTOBER 2015   NOVEMBER 2015   DECEMBER 2015

Last roof cranes
dismantled.

19 JANUARY

3 FEBRUARY

JANUARY 2016

FEBRUARY 2016

Arrival of the first elements of the
organ. They weigh approximately
4 tons out of an eventual total of 25.

Presentation of the 'white skin'.

Left: the voicing of the organ is completed at the end of June. Above: for the first time, the 'white skin' in the Grand Hall can be properly seen. Below: the chairs—made in Italy—are installed.

31 MARCH   **11 APRIL**   **15 APRIL**

MARCH 2016   APRIL 2016   MAY 2016

Hamburg parliament approves operating plan for the Elbphilharmonie and the Laeiszhalle.

General artistic director Christoph Lieben-Seutter presents his programme for the opening season.

The NDR Sinfonieorchester is renamed the NDR Elbphilharmonie Orchester.

Workers take more than two years to install the 10,000 panels making up the 'white skin', every one of them different. This will be a key factor in the Grand Hall's extraordinary acoustics.

20 JUNE

30 JUNE

JUNE 2016

JULY 2016

Tickets go on sale for the first concerts at the Elbphilharmonie.

Handover of Elbphilharmonie concert area to the city of Hamburg.

2 SEPTEMBER

AUGUST 2016   SEPTEMBER 2016   OCTOBER 2016

First 'technical rehearsal' of the NDR Elbphilharmonie Orchester in the Grand Hall, in the presence of First Mayor Olaf Scholz and acoustician Yasuhisa Toyota. Scores on the music stands include, among others, Brahms' First and Mendelssohn's Fourth.

A charming character: the
Elbphilharmonie rises
imposingly above the roofs of
Hamburg, all other buildings
pale into insignificance.

31 OCTOBER 4 NOVEMBER

11 JANUARY

NOVEMBER 2016

DECEMBER 2016

Contractually-agreed date
of handover of the building
to the city of Hamburg.

Gala opening of the Plaza
to the public.

Inaugural concert with the NDR Elbphilharmonie
Orchester, under the leadership of principal conductor
Thomas Hengelbrock.

'THE ELBPHILHARMONIE IS VERY DEAR TO US. IN BOTH SENSES OF THE WORD.'

CULTURE SENATOR **BARBARA KISSELER** HAS A SENSE OF HUMOUR ABOUT THE CONSTRUCTION PROBLEMS, 15 JUNE 2011.

THE ROCKY ROAD

S ydney Opera House's initial price tag came to a reasonable enough sum: A$7 million. In a flurry of great optimism, building work began in 1959, aiming for completion in 1963. What followed were innumerable crises, arguments, and the eventual sacking of the Danish architect Jørn Utzon. However, eventually the grand opening was indeed celebrated—in 1973. The final cost: A$102 million. In 2003, Utzon received the Pritzker Prize for his life's work, two years after Jacques Herzog and Pierre de Meuron had won. Four years later, UNESCO added the famous Sydney 'shells' to its list of World Heritage Sites. And to put all this into perspective, it took 632 years for Cologne Cathedral to take the form we know today. Put into that wider context, Hamburg has done quite well in building the Elbphilharmonie. Delays have been shorter, and costs to city taxpayers 'only' increased threefold, rising from almost €272 million to €789 million. But, of course, this is hardly anything to brag about.

When Christian Wulff, then president of Germany, visited the construction site in June 2011, Culture Senator Barbara Kisseler humorously summed up the project's woes in two sentences: 'The Elbphilharmonie is very dear to us. In both senses of the word.' Cicero, the political magazine, called the new architectural jewel the 'world's most beautiful tax sinkhole'. The news magazine Der Spiegel, based here in Hamburg, was even crueller in its broadside: it dubbed the building 'Neuschwanstein on the Elbe', alluding to the vast folly of a castle built by Ludwig II, the ruinously extravagant King of Bavaria.

Looking back, maybe it was the early euphoria surrounding the project which led to things getting so complicated so quickly, with all those nasty costs and contradictory interpretations of what was going on. Back then, the concept of the Elbphilharmonie seemed to have fallen from the sky from one day to the next. It was there, fully formed. And it all sounded so marvellous, so enticing. Not simple, definitely not simple. But doable. Somehow. Anyone who has ever fallen head-over-heels in love knows how easy it is to turn a blind eye to unpleasant truths. Until later down the road, when those unpleasant truths risk blocking out the rest of the view.

In Hamburg—as in Sydney decades before—plans were announced, contracts awarded and work was begun, long before the plans had really been fully elaborated. Which is why, in far too many areas, the stated costs were little more than ballpark figures and couldn't be taken at face value. Then, in 2007, to make things even worse, another contract was worked out. If anything, this one resulted in a whole load more trouble and sent costs spiralling. To put it in simple terms: Partner A (the city) would commission B (the architects) to undertake the planning. But A would also commission C (the construction firm, Hochtief). However, B and C were under no contractual obligation to each other and they would soon have different ideas as to what had to be built—and when.

And so the buck was passed, back and forth and side to side, because there were always more loopholes for it to be passed through. While one side was trying to implement one thing, the other side decided to come up with something entirely new— and then expected the others to comply. Each party was working to its own timetable. Complaints, cost overruns and changes began to pile up. A great big Bermuda Triangle had been created, and it soon began to swallow up architectural plans, illusory cost estimates, and a string of planned opening dates that came—and went.

In those early years, arguments and problems accumulated. So did prices. They shot through the roof even before there was a roof. And there was very little that did not set off arguments: triggers included everything from toilet brushes to ventilation ducting. At the very beginning, relations were friendly and untroubled. But not for long. In an alarming number of areas, the companies involved had simply not laid down detailed specifications. Instead, they relied on vague plans, in the misplaced faith that Hochtief had been contracted at a fixed overall rate, and so it would have an incentive to keep costs down. On top of all that were some very problematic arrangements for the financing of the restaurant, hotel and parking garage. In November 2006, Ole von Beust, then First Mayor of Hamburg, announced a final figure of €241.3 million in construction costs, assuring the public that the city's part of

that bill was capped at €114.3 million. At this point, the public remained in the dark about the costs to be borne by the city for the construction of the hotel, restaurant and parking garage (totalling €129.4 million), as well as the €28 million in planning costs incurred by the architects and ReGe. On 28 February 2007, the Bürgerschaft, Hamburg's parliament, unanimously green-lighted the project. But only a month after the contract was signed, the first amendments to it were being drawn up. One day before the (purely symbolic) ground-breaking cere-mony, the project manager in charge threw in the towel. Then in June 2008, the city's Culture Senator, Karin von Welck, had to be the bearer of some bad news. A first delay—the Philhar-monie would only open in the autumn of 2011. In November 2008, there was a further package of bad news, the so-called 'Amendment 4': costs to the taxpayer had purportedly shot up again, this time to the tune of €495 million. To sugar the pill a little, at the same time a brand new and final—supposedly—opening date was announced: doors would open in early 2012. In April 2010, the city of Hamburg took the main construction company to court, to force them at long last to produce a workable schedule. One month later, the first of two parlia-mentary committees of investigation began hearings. In the meantime, the grand opening was postponed yet again, this time to the beginning of 2013. In early 2011, a second parliamentary inquiry took up more or less where the first had left off. That one had been halted by the local elections held after the collapse of the city's Christian Democrat–Green coalition government. Half a year after the building's topping-out ceremony, hopes were fading fast that Hamburg and Hochtief could put their heads together and resolve their differences outside a courtroom. Yet again, another absolutely-positively final date for a grand opening was put off—this time until November 2013.

In June 2011, the handover date was postponed until April 2014. Then, in October 2011, construction work came almost to a complete standstill, since the contractor Hochtief judged that the roof construction was not solid enough to lower it into its final position. Each party understood the situation very differently. While this went on, the handover date was again postponed: November 2014 became the latest 100 per cent-certain, no-question-about-it final date. The city government was on the warpath. On more than one warpath, in fact. Fol-lowing all the missed deadlines, they demanded a fine of €40 million from the construction firm.

OLAF SCHOLZ
FIRST MAYOR OF THE FREE HANSEATIC
CITY OF HAMBURG

Serious financial planning and watertight contracts form the solid basis of every construction project. But that is far from what lawyer Olaf Scholz found when he took office at City Hall. From March 2011 onwards, Scholz was the driving force for the renegotiation of the contract. With the 2013 signing there was, for the first time, a contract without ifs and buts—six years after construction began. 'We have no more risks,' said the SPD politician with satisfaction. This was in accordance with his motto of 'proper governance'. It is also what made Scholz's slip of the tongue in January 2015 during the official announcement of the opening date so amusing: although he had the date of 11 January on the tip of his tongue, he faltered before correctly naming the year, 2017.

WHAT THE ELBPHILHARMONIE COST

This outline was arrived at using several calculations. Among other things, it includes costs, donations, revenues and fees. In this way, we get an overall picture of the sums invested and spent on the building over the years, since the earliest planning began.

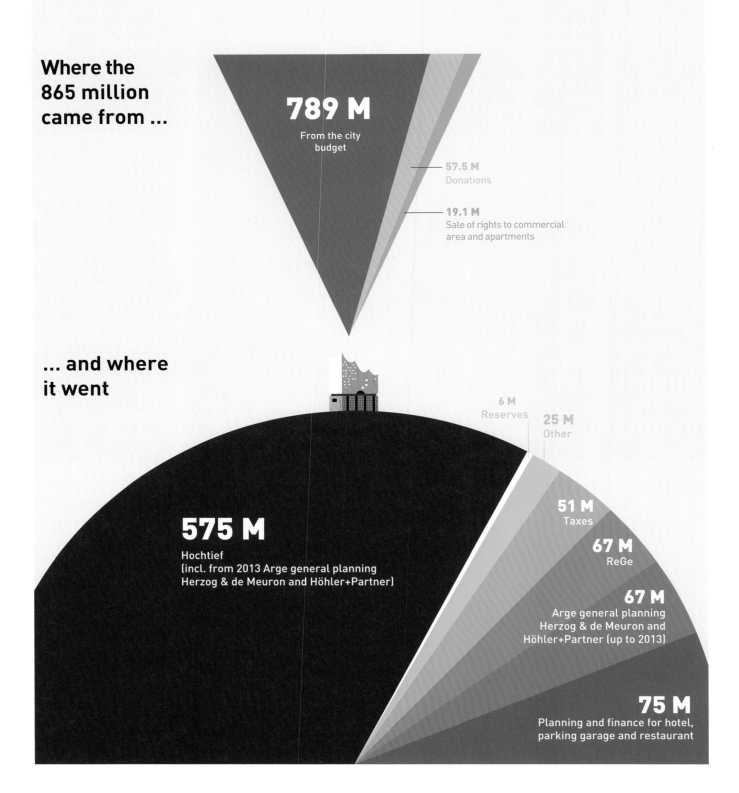

Where the
865 million
came from ...

789 M
From the city
budget

57.5 M
Donations

19.1 M
Sale of rights to commercial
area and apartments

... and where
it went

6 M
Reserves

25 M
Other

575 M
Hochtief
(incl. from 2013 Arge general planning
Herzog & de Meuron and Höhler+Partner)

51 M
Taxes

67 M
ReGe

67 M
Arge general planning
Herzog & de Meuron and
Höhler+Partner (up to 2013)

75 M
Planning and finance for hotel,
parking garage and restaurant

Early in 2012, the city presented Hochtief with an ultimatum: the company was told to recommence construction and finish lowering the roof by 31 May, or see the entire contract ripped up. In response, Hochtief kept on building, but did not lower the roof. A series of further ultimatums followed. In September, safety measurements were carried out on the outer surface of the roof and on the steel support structure. Olaf Scholz announced that a solution would be found by Christmas. The politicians won this round too: at the end of November, the roof was lowered and attached to the rest of the building. And—believe it or not—nothing terrible happened. Except to the date of opening, which was postponed again, this time to early 2016. While all this was going on, the Elbphilharmonie's general artistic director, Christoph Lieben-Seutter, who should by now have been celebrating two years of musical direction in the building, as had been foreseen when he took office in 2007, was making plans for concerts in the Laeiszhalle instead.

Just before Christmas 2012, the First Mayor and Culture Senator presented a lovely gift to the city: after days of tough negotiations, existing contracts were dumped and the entire disastrous confusion was emphatically ended. From now on, the city would have a single direct contract with Hochtief. The architects would be responsible for 'overall artistic direction' and quality control. They would now have contracts with the building firm, which would bear all future risks. All problems were to be sorted out directly between Hochtief and Herzog & de Meuron. 'There has never been a contract like this,' said a jubilant Olaf Scholz, 'we have no more risks.' The only alternative was for the city to get rid of Hochtief, spend years fighting it out in the courts over compensation payments, and take charge of the continuing construction work itself. The new deal meant this grim fallback was definitively off the table. As a result of this agreement, the final handover date was again postponed, to the end of October 2016. The grand opening was pencilled in for January 2017. But the biggest problem now was not time, but money: the overall price had continued to spiral steeply upward. So for the new agreement, the city's principle was 'better safe than sorry': building costs were renamed the blissfully tautological 'Total Blanket Fixed Price' and a maximum figure was set at €575 million. Overall expenditure on the building rose to €866 million, with the city paying €789 million of that figure. By early 2013, the new contracts were ready to be signed. Hochtief abandoned all additional demands, and the city waived millions in possible compensation claims. The time of arguments and lawsuits was to be definitively ended by this new 'blanket' deal. 'This new arrangement is a marriage of convenience, not of love. But we all know marriages of convenience last longer,' commented the Culture Senator on the happy ending.

On 9 April 2013, six years and one week after the ground-breaking ceremonial, the new contracts were signed. 'We've included everything we could think of,' Olaf Scholz, the First Mayor, was glad to remark, now with both hands firmly gripping the purse strings. 'As far as we know, we've left nothing out.' At the launch of the feasibility study in June 2005, almost eight years previously, his predecessor Ole von Beust had confidently announced that the city's share of the costs would be no more than €77 million. And that, he said, 'is a very conservative estimate'. He went on: 'I am convinced that the taxpayers' share will actually be considerably less than that.' €77 million was the 'absolute limit', he promised. It was a mistake of historic proportions, which returned again and again to haunt those in charge of the project and of the city. Over the years, as each successive cost increase was announced, von Beust's blithe early claim was repeatedly quoted, like an unwanted echo. But a lot has happened since then. The change in mood surrounding the project began with a gradual waning of negative headlines. Then the opening date began to grow nearer, looming close enough to actually imagine. Gradually it became clear that the project was actually going to be completed, that soon the Elbphilharmonie would emerge, grabbing the attention of music lovers around the world. Bad publicity and ridicule also began to ebb away. Now there was actually something physically there for Hamburg to be proud of, a new and palpable sense of ease and anticipation emerged in the city, a feeling of 'Well, there you go! It worked out after all!' In the summer of 2012, during the period of greatest frustration, general artistic director Christoph Lieben-Seutter spoke of the Elbphilharmonie as a 'laughing stock' around the world. Early in 2016, Die Süddeutsche Zeitung, a newspaper from Munich, a city which has long tried and failed to develop a new concert hall, wrote about the building they had once referred to as the 'concert ha-ha-hall' and as 'the catastrophe, the effrontery, the madness' on the Elbe. Now the newspaper came to a different conclusion: the Elbphilharmonie, which had begun as the 'stupidest building site in the world', had become something fantastic, 'not only despite its history, but because of it'.

'WE'VE INCLUDED EVERYTHING WE COULD THINK OF. AS FAR AS WE KNOW, WE'VE LEFT NOTHING OUT.'

FIRST MAYOR **OLAF SCHOLZ**
ON THE FINAL CONTRACT
BETWEEN THE CITY
AND HOCHTIEF, THE
CONSTRUCTION COMPANY

THE KAISERKAI: A STREET THROUGH TIME

In May 2004, fresh tarmac cuts directly through the sandy wasteland of the docks. Kaispeicher A stands huge, a vast hulking mass. Six years later, HafenCity is flourishing with offices, cafés and apartments, with the Elbphilharmonie rising to meet the sky. Today almost nothing is left from those previous times. The concert hall at the end of the street has arrived right in the middle of the city.

MAY 2004

MAY 2010

MAY 2015

CHRISTOPH LIEBEN-SEUTTER
GENERAL DIRECTOR OF THE
ELBPHILHARMONIE AND THE LAEISZHALLE

The decision to leave Vienna, the world capital of
classical music, for the post of 'cultural developmen-
tal aid worker' and the chance of giving the merchant
city of Hamburg a new musical identity was an
unusual career move, particularly for an Austrian.
What the new general director of the Elbphilharmonie
and the Laeiszhalle found on the banks of the Elbe in
2007 was more than a construction site with an
uncertain future: his contract was set for five years,
and the concert house was scheduled to open three
years after he assumed his post. In the end it took ten
years, during which time Christoph Lieben-Seutter
served as director of one concert house while
devising plans for another. In July 2016 his contract
was renewed until 2021.

Tour

The Elbphilharmonie is full of
surprises that no other concert hall
comes close to offering.

In these pages you'll find
fascinating details about all areas of the
building and a behind-the-scenes
look at the luxury hotel and
apartments with their unspoilt
view of the Elbe and Alster.

THE ELBPHILHARMONIE IS SO MUCH MORE THAN A CONCERT HALL.

Its heart and emotional core are the various concert halls behind glass. It also boasts eateries and parking spaces, and a plaza from where visitors can enjoy a panoramic view of Hamburg. The building complex on the banks of the Elbe also contains a luxury hotel and apartments on its western edge.

1 The building
A sculpture in stone and glass

2 Car park
A launchpad for the music

3 Tube
Take the Tube to music heaven

4 Plaza
Terrace with views of the Elbe

5 Acoustics
Yasuhisa Toyota's search for the ideal concert hall

6 Grand Hall
Gesamtkunstwerk balancing functionality and effect

7 Recital Hall
Character is never a question of size

8 Kaistudios
An education in music

9 Hotel
Room with a concert

10 Apartments
Very close to heaven

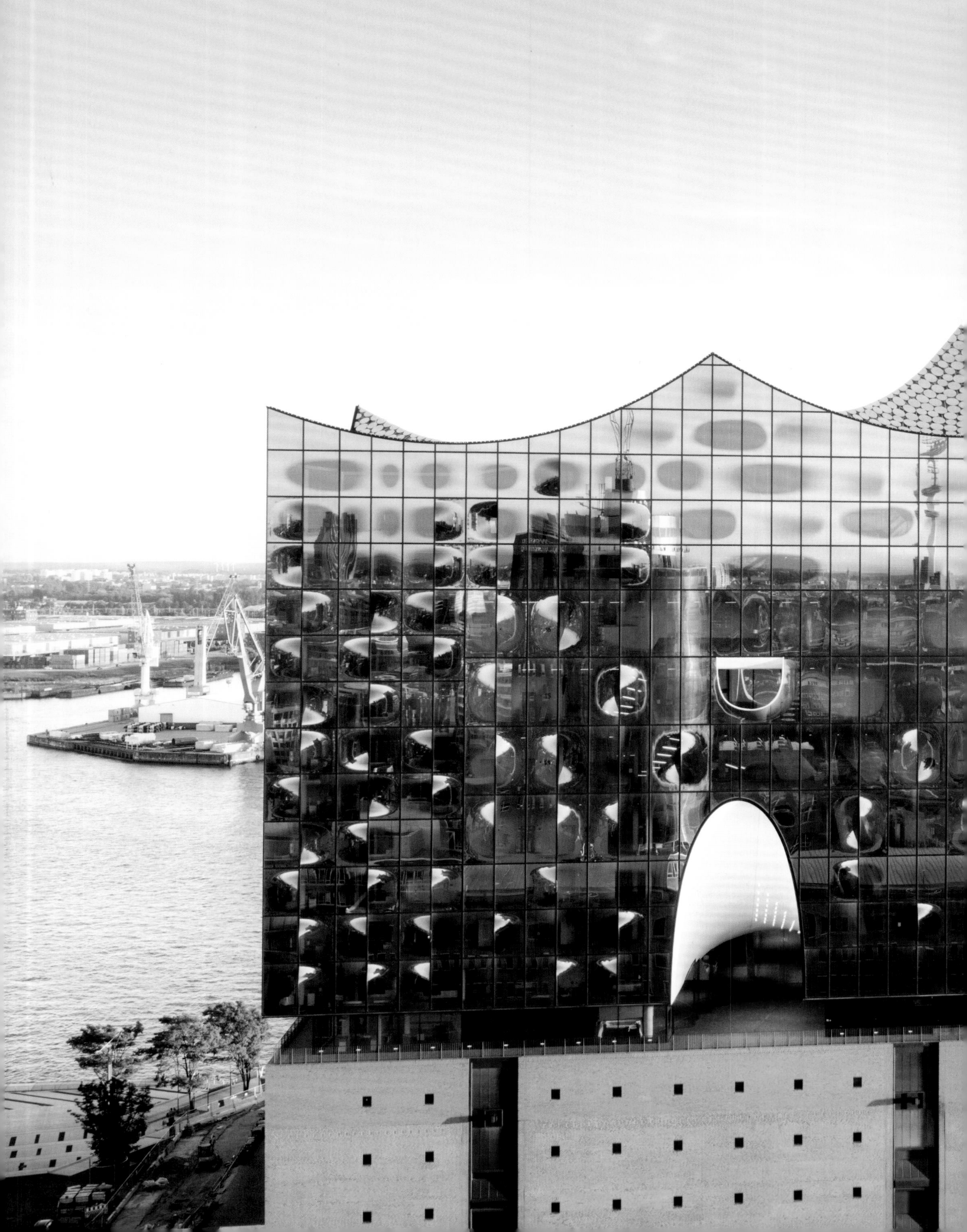

BUILDING USE

117 841 m² total floor space

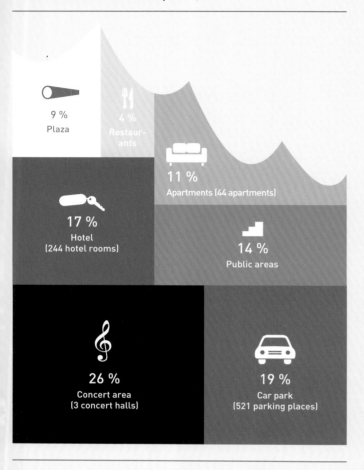

- 9 % Plaza
- 4 % Restaurants
- 11 % Apartments (44 apartments)
- 17 % Hotel (244 hotel rooms)
- 14 % Public areas
- 26 % Concert area (3 concert halls)
- 19 % Car park (521 parking places)

82 m is the length of the arched escalator, the longest in Europe

CORRESPONDS TO

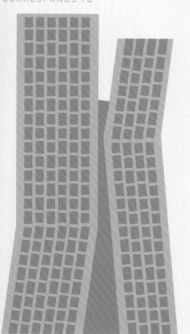

29

total number of elevators

11

staircases

CONCERT AREA

Grand Hall

2091 seats

CORRESPONDS TO

approx. the size of the Grand Hall in the Laeiszhalle

approx. **3300 m²**

CORRESPONDS TO

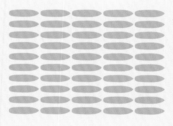

about 50 Alster Ships

approx. **25 m** high

CORRESPONDS TO

ceiling

17.8 m
highest seat

a stack of all the elephants at Tierpark Hagenbeck

Recital Hall

approx. **550** seats

CORRESPONDS TO

approx. the size of the Recital Hall in the Laeiszhalle

462.71 m²

CORRESPONDS TO

about 7 Alster Ships

Kaistudio 1

308.28 m²

CORRESPONDS TO

about 5 Alster Ships

approx. **170** seats

CORRESPONDS TO

approx. the size of Studio E in the Laeiszhalle

BUILDING DIMENSIONS

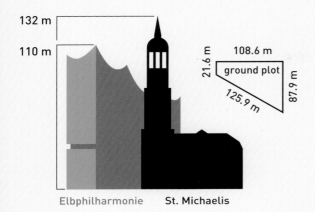

132 m
110 m

Elbphilharmonie   St. Michaelis

21.6 m
108.6 m
ground plot
125.9 m
87.9 m

approx. 120 000 m² in surface area

CORRESPONDS TO

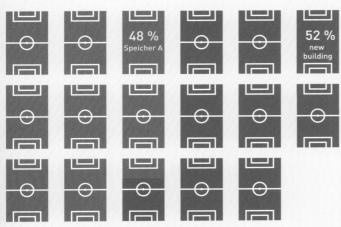

48 %
Speicher A

52 %
new building

17 times the size of FC St. Pauli's football pitch

approx. 200 000 t total weight

CORRESPONDS TO

30 times the weight of the Cap San Diego

MATERIALS USED

approx. 18 000 t of steel

CORRESPONDS TO

the weight of about 32 Airbus A380 aeroplanes

63 000 m³ of concrete

CORRESPONDS TO

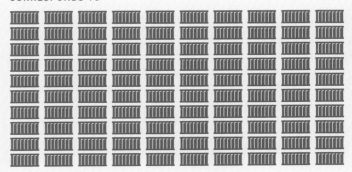

the volume of approx. 100 large shipping containers

2200 shaped glass panes

CORRESPONDS TO

roughly the number of bridges in Hamburg

1.8 t is the weight of a two-pane glass element

CORRESPONDS TO

twice the weight of the millennium bell in St. Michaelis

Skyscraper: the view to the top of
the building offers a feeling for its
dimensions and illustrates the
contrast of old and new.

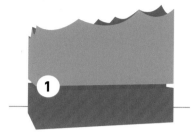

A SCULPTURE IN STONE AND GLASS

The smallest and most beloved unit of architectural success in Hamburg is not the many euros one somehow managed to save during the building process. No, it is the brick.

Brick is the material that lends St. Michaelis—affectionately dubbed 'the Michel'—and the Laeiszhalle their character. And it is definitely no coincidence that Hamburg's two very own World Heritage Sites—Chile House and the Speicherstadt—are brick-built classics. Kaispeicher A is another brick-clad building. The aesthetic tension of the Elbphilharmonie building is created by the contrast, symbolic and material, between raw, red old brick below and smooth reflective modernity on top.

That skilful stylistic rupture, implemented to the highest quality, is typical of the philosophy of Herzog & de Meuron, the Elbphilharmonie's architects. The brick base has a certain simplicity, a modesty, which stands in marked contrast to the waves of glass rising up from the Plaza.

A reminder of the old building's function can be seen on its east side. Where once large letters spelled out KAISPEICHER A, now the same DIN 1451 font, the same 52 centimetre-high letters, announce the ELBPHILHARMONIE. Painted in silk-matt 'traffic white' on a red background, the letters send out a clear signal: this building is a product of German workmanship. Another historical allusion can be found on the south side—three gantry cranes which once heaved goods onto dry land. Now a relic of the port's history and protected monuments. The construction work meant raising the existing roof of Kaispeicher A by five metres, in order to preserve the original proportions. As a result, the final layer of brick below the Plaza is no longer entirely original, but faithfully modelled on the original brickwork. Any brick damaged during construction work was returned to pristine condition by experts who worked on the restoration of Dresden's war-damaged Frauenkirche.

A mountain range in the north-German flatland: you can't get much closer to the skies over Hamburg than on the sequin-pattern roof. The view from the Kühne Sky Lounge, named after patron Klaus-Michael Kühne, is utterly unique.

Special effects: the sequin-pattern roof and glass
facades play with light and shadow to brilliant effect.

The best view of the giant glass sequins on the roof is from a
passing aeroplane. This, the 'building's fifth facade', has a
shape that somehow combines crystal and sail, wave and
peak. Thanks to its singular surface, the building's appearance
is never stable; it constantly shifts and changes. Approach in
misty morning light from the Fischmarkt, and you'll behold a
vast opaque colossus. In bright sunlight, seen from a boat on
the river, the building gleams like a glass sculpture. On warm
summer evenings, it reaches into the blue sky, sublime. After
darkness has fallen, it shines invitingly, lit from within, each
window a little question mark. It almost seems like you can
see right through and into the building. One thing is certain—
the last thing this building engenders is indifference.

The facade's glass-pane jigsaw puzzle was put together by
the firm Joseph Gartner, based in Gundelfingen in southwest
Germany, and famous for dealing with special requests and
difficult cases from all over the world, including BMW World
in Munich, the Museum of Modern Art in New York, and the
Norman-Foster-designed 'Apple Campus 2', in Cupertino,
California.

Endurance testing for composite safety glass is a serious
business: the panels are tested against heat, cold and,
crucially for this location, against driving rain and 150 kilo-
metres/hour winds—their taster for Hamburg's notorious
'Schietwetter', stormy weather.

Another stress test is the 'pendulum impact' which tests the
glass panels' endurance against random powerful impacts.
Here, the role of a malevolent outside force is played by a set
of double tyres, weighing a full 50 kilogrammes, which are
mechanically thumped against the panels at various points.
On this occasion, one American material-testing method was
not used: over there, they've been known to shoot lengths of

wood at buildings with a bazooka. But Joseph Gartner brought an equally impressive testing device: a fourteen-cylinder double-star radial engine. Built in 1959, the engine has 2,200 horsepower and can shoot two litres of water per square metre per minute at the glass facade.

The printed dot configuration on the exterior surface of many of the facade's double-glazed panels is not just a whimsical design detail. Those grey dots also minimize the intensity of sunlight. Around one third of all the glass used on the building has this dot pattern. A reflective chrome layer and an insulation layer intensify the luminous effect.

After the architects abandoned their original idea of a flat facade, the new key shapes—resembling fish gills and horse-shoes—presented a whole new set of challenges for the glazing team. After the dots had been applied with millimetre precision, each glass panel was bent into shape at 600°C, formed into the curves, bulges, and gigantic tuning forks which lend visual variety to the facade. Nothing like this had ever been done before. The mounting of the panels began on 16 December 2009 and continued until early 2011. But it was not until three years later—at 1.21 pm on 31 January 2014, in freezing weather—that the last of the 1,096 glass pieces was officially inserted into the facade. By then, 16,000 square metres had been glazed over, equivalent to 3,830 table-tennis tables.

The Elbphilharmonie's next unique feature is its roof con-struction. This also called for precision work: eight concave sections covering 6,000 square metres and weighing a total of 8,000 tons. The lowest point of the undulating roof is 79.1 metres above the river, the highest 110 metres. It is supported by around 1,000 struts, each one individually shaped and welded, forming a small mountain range here on the flat North German Plain. One clever side-effect of the sloping construction: it helps rainwater drain off more easily.

This forest of struts had a toughened glazed surface laid on top, composed of a layer of 10,000 giant white aluminium sequins, each with a diameter of 90 or 110 centimetres. The perforation pattern created echoes of the pattern of the facade: 3D digital design meant the sequins could be positioned with exceptional precision, so they form a single unbroken design, in spite of their different sizes. At their steepest, the roof's waves have an angle of 51 degrees. The roof's wave-pattern is interrupted in three places: twice by light shafts—one on the east side for the apartments, one on

the west for the hotel—and once by a terrace for concert-goers, around 75 metres up on the south-east corner of the building.

Under the Elbphilharmonie's roof yet more cutting-edge technology can be found, in the form of 2.7 kilometres of ventilation shafts, up to three metres in diameter, which pass invisibly through the building. All told, the shafts weigh around 900 tons, and allow around 65,000 cubic metres of air to circulate through the building. In the event of a fire, smoke extraction technology can take out ten times that amount from the concert hall.

On 15 August 2014, precisely according to the new schedule laid down in the restructuring agreement, the roof of the Elbphilharmonie was sealed, with almost all of the remaining under-roof work already completed. Look at it any way you want: this building's interior fulfils the promise of its exterior.

Left: inside the lighting remains constant, but the external appearance changes from one moment to the next. The glass makes the facades appear to change colour, depending on sunlight and weather conditions.

Where once sacks of cocoa were piled up high, now concert-goers park their cars.

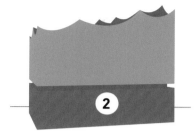

A LAUNCHPAD FOR THE MUSIC

There can't be many car parks in the world which have witnessed a multimedia performance of Igor Stravinsky's pulsing, energy-filled masterpiece 'Le Sacre du Printemps'. It was general artistic director Christoph Lieben-Seutter who had an unusual staging idea for this very unusual location. As he put it: 'If the concert hall isn't ready, then we'll play in the building site.' So it was that in May 2013, in Kaispeicher A, where the building's 521 parking spaces now stand, Lieben-Seutter put on a virtual guest performance by the London Philharmonia and its then principal conductor Esa-Pekka Salonen. The 're-rite' concept saw video-screens and music stands distributed throughout the semi-darkness of the car park. Visitors could observe individual instruments, conduct along with Salonen, and have a close-up experience of how the individual parts of Stravinsky's masterpiece fit together.

Over the years, there have been many changes in the plans for the new glass building above the Plaza. But the brick building underneath has also had its share of revision and refinement. The powers that be eventually discarded the idea of putting a space for alternative culture alongside the car park, opting instead for an eatery. In the final version of the Kaispeicher, the car park's neighbours include wellness and conference facilities for the hotel, the music education area with its seven Kaistudios, storage areas, and backstage facilities for the two concert halls.

The car park is unusual simply by virtue of its location: very few concert halls can offer parking within the building itself. Herzog & de Meuron here went for contrast: the materials chosen for the facade, the Grand Hall and the Plaza are all hard, intentionally so. But down below, there are no pressed glass panes, no panelling shaped to the millimetre. Bare concrete sets the tone here, and the launch pad to the music is a spiral shaft that takes cars higher and higher, up into the structure.

Well-rounded: the spiral ramp of the parking garage links the levels inside the Kaispeicher.

Overture in warm grey: the price of admission includes this spectacular ride on the vaulted escalator.

TUBE

TAKE THE TUBE TO MUSIC HEAVEN

The Tube is much too fast to use Led Zeppelin's 'Stairway to Heaven' as background music. The 1971 rock ballad is eight whole minutes long, whereas the Tube will get you up to the Plaza in just two and a half. But the escalator isn't just an outstanding architectural achievement. It is also a metaphor: it reliably brings people up and away from the ground of their everyday lives; in just a few minutes, the uplifting experience takes them to a different level of consciousness; and all this in a building which owes its very existence to another one below.

The two-lane, convex-arch escalator is 82 metres long: at the bottom, the passenger cannot see where it ends, 21.43 metres higher up. Like many of the Elbphilharmonie's technical achievements, the escalator demanded precision work. And it is special enough to get a name of its own: the Tube. The Tube was developed and built by the Finnish company Kone. The smooth, shaft-like tunnel walls, reminiscent of an auditory canal, are coloured a delicate, warm grey, and decorated with 7,900 glass sequins which reflect and refract the light.

To intensify the effect, the tunnel tapers at the apex of its curve, then widens enticingly until it arrives at the sixth floor. Here visitors can stop off on the west side of the building, where they are greeted by a quintessentially Hamburg panorama: looking directly into the sunset, they have an unbroken view of the river towards the St. Pauli Piers.

Originally, a canteen was planned for the large gap in the brickwork on the west side of Kaispeicher A. But it failed to gain planning permission. At the top of the first escalator, dining facilities await visitors. The next escalator they take leads further up towards the Plaza on level eight. And here the final leg of the journey is done without mechanical assistance—up a wide ramp built of classic red brick. Welcome to the Elbphilharmonie.

Halfway to the finishing line: a waypoint en route to the Plaza is impressive for its design.

When it isn't moving, the large escalator has around 200 steps in each of its lanes. When fully loaded with adults, each weighing on average 75 kilogrammes, the Tube has to move a weight of around 30 tons. But to cope with any eventuality, the escalator's machinery is designed to withstand 120 kilogrammes per step. The five motors each produce fifteen watts of energy, seven and a half times more than a normal department-store escalator. They also power the 165-metre long handrail (weighing 300 kilogrammes on each side). All five motors are synchronized and equipped with speed sensors. To cope with the post-concert rush, the direction of the escalators is reversed and the descent can be sped up to 0.63 metres per second. Work on this crucial element of the building was at a standstill for three whole years: the first attempt to finish the escalator left hundreds of cracks in the plaster, spoiling the overall effect.

You can always take one of the lifts to the upper levels of the building. But if you take the Tube, even just getting to the concert becomes an extraordinary experience in itself.

Dramatic experience: the view from the Kaispeicher's panorama window looks out to the St. Pauli Piers.

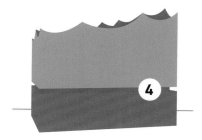

TERRACE WITH VIEWS OF THE ELBE

The Plaza is much more than just a concert-hall foyer. The Plaza is the Elbphilharmonie's visiting card, a symbol for everything the building believes in, everything it thinks it should offer the world. 'Here all the characteristics of the building's interior come together,' says Barbara Kisseler, Hamburg's Senator of Culture, lauding the Plaza as 'pure poetry in architecture, but with very specific Hamburg roots'. Herzog & de Meuron's architect Ascan Mergenthaler calls the Plaza an 'interface and distribution centre'. He adds: 'You feel the weight of the past and the strength of the warehouse below us, and then sense the festive world above.'

The Plaza is the transitional area between the heavy stone of Kaispeicher A and the glass wave above. Quite simply, this is where visitors and hotel guests arrive, to a space as large as Hamburg's City Hall Square, the Rathausmarkt. The basic idea in the building's philosophy is that this Plaza is for everyone. You don't need concert tickets: the Plaza invites everyone to come and stroll around in its wide spaces. After the escalator journey through the arched Tube to the sixth floor, then the second escalator to the eighth floor (the less spectacular alternative is to take one of the eleven lifts) here is where the building greets its visitors and puts them in the mood for further attractions, including 4,400 square metres of premium living space in a magnificent river location with an unbeatable view.

The location offers a panoramic view over the city, thanks to a walkway which goes right round the Plaza, the full circumference of the building. Which makes the Elbphilharmonie the world's only 360 degree viewing tower with a house orchestra! Far below, the city lies at your feet—the container port, the docks, the church towers, the view of the city centre, the whole breadth of the metropolis. It doesn't get more Hamburg than this. The entrance portals to the walkway are two huge wind deflectors, six metres high and

The ascent to the Plaza is the last step before the open space and the large entryways to the two concert halls.

Ear canal: the great staircase leading to the Grand Hall.

studio ↓ rkhaus

Both eye-catching and wind-catching:
curved 'glass curtains' mark the
entrance to the Plaza's open-air areas.

two and a half metres wide, free-standing curtains made of curved safety glass, one each in front of the northern and southern sections of the walkway. Look down, and you'll see another distinctive feature of the Plaza. Like the outer walls of Kaispeicher A, the ground here is formed of bricks, almost 188,000 of them, fired in the kilns of Germany's Münster region, with every tenth brick bearing the emblem of the town of Gescher—a bell.

There is even underfloor heating: in autumn and winter it can get very cold up here, thirty-seven metres above the water. The space is dominated by the steel-and-concrete stairways leading down to the foyers of the Grand Hall and the Recital Hall. With their curved form, these stairways are also reminiscent of parts of the ear. The views up to the concert hall foyers stimulate visitors' curiosity about the auditoria up there, hidden behind soundproof walls.

Long before the building was completed, the Plaza was the location for its first public concert. Very early in the development, the Ensemble Resonanz performed its work 'Enter the Kaispeicher!' in the raw surroundings of the old port building, marking the building with a cultural scent as a sign of things to come. Then, in September 2012, the 'German Requiem' by Johannes Brahms, a Hamburger by birth, was performed in the construction site of the Plaza. The performance was as special as the location: Hamburg Theatre Festival invited the Berlin Radialsystem's 'human requiem' production to Hamburg. In this 'three-dimensional concert version' of the piece, the singers of the Berliner Rundfunkchor, wearing everyday clothing, moved around among the 800 spectators. The piano, conductor and co-conductor were also placed amidst the audience. The members of the choir sat on swings to sing 'Wie lieblich sind Deine Wohnungen, Herr Zebaoth'. Roll-out grass turf, sandbags and piles of building materials formed the backdrop to a theatrical prayer held in the midst of raw concrete. Biblical quotations were hung from the columns; during 'Selig sind die Toten', the lights were extinguished.

At the topping-out ceremony on 28 May 2010, Ole von Beust, the First Mayor of Hamburg, said of the panoramic view: 'From here you can see Hamburg's soul'. Commenting on his long wait for construction to finish so his work as general artistic director could properly begin, Christoph Lieben-Seutter quoted the German proverb: 'Good things take their own time'. The senior foreman managed to give everyone a fright by

knocking over the traditional glass of schnapps as he spoke the time-honoured verse: 'After many hard blows, after many hard days' work, with diligence and care, we have completed our proud work, and look – how splendid this building is.' The schnapps should be drunk and the glass thrown from the roof. If it breaks, it signifies good luck.

On the day, the representatives of the city government, the architects and the building companies tactfully concealed their own ongoing struggles. For weeks before and after the ceremony, relations were far less pleasant than on the day itself, with all three sides caught up in arguments over cost estimates and seriously delayed schedules. Meanwhile, down at ground level, demonstrators from the Recht auf Stadt ('Right to the City') movement staged a protest: they wore Roman clothing and handed out €350 million banknotes, condemning what they saw as the project's 'decadence'. A river launch even got in on the complaint, displaying an 'Enter the Elphi' placard. Nonetheless, only days later, the 4,000 tickets available for a tour of the building site were sold out in just three hours.

The large columns in the Plaza, all of varying thickness, are not vertical. This is not a mistake on the part of the draughtsman. It's intentional: the structural engineers placed the columns with great precision, designing them to carry the enormous weight of the new building above them, then pass it on towards the earth.

Positioned in such a way that no one column stands directly on the periphery, the columns create the impression that the new construction hovers over the old brick warehouse. Right angles are in any case rare in this building, something that did not make life any easier for the builders. The curved ceiling absorbs sound: its undulations can also be seen as mirroring the curves of the building's roof. And hidden away behind the ceiling are 320 metres of walkways for maintenance personnel to use.

As everywhere in the Elbphilharmonie, the detail in the Plaza is astonishing: the blown-glass lamps far above the Plaza are coated very precisely to provide optimal lighting without dazzling those strolling below. In the foyers, long light fixtures are arranged so they function as directional signs, pointing directly to the spot in the Grand Hall where the conductor's podium stands. The Elbphilharmonie, in other words, has a light-signage system which takes guests right to where the music is.

The variety of forms and materials
on the Plaza creates dramatic
transitions to the exterior.

Soundscape: the harbour and the Elbe define the setting of the concert house. The terrace surrounds the Plaza, offering visitors the possibility of walking the entire perimeter of the Elbphilharmonie and views in every direction.

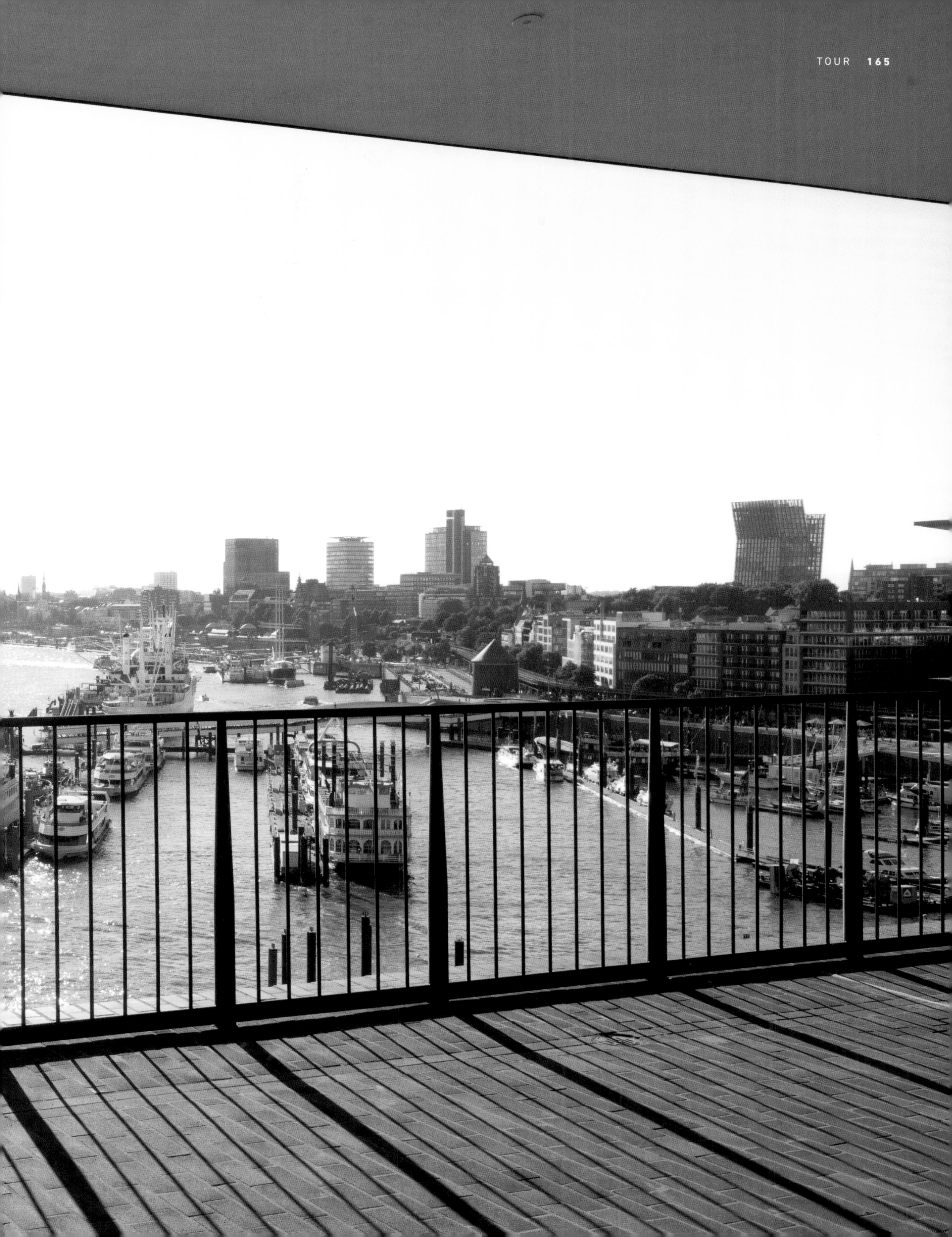

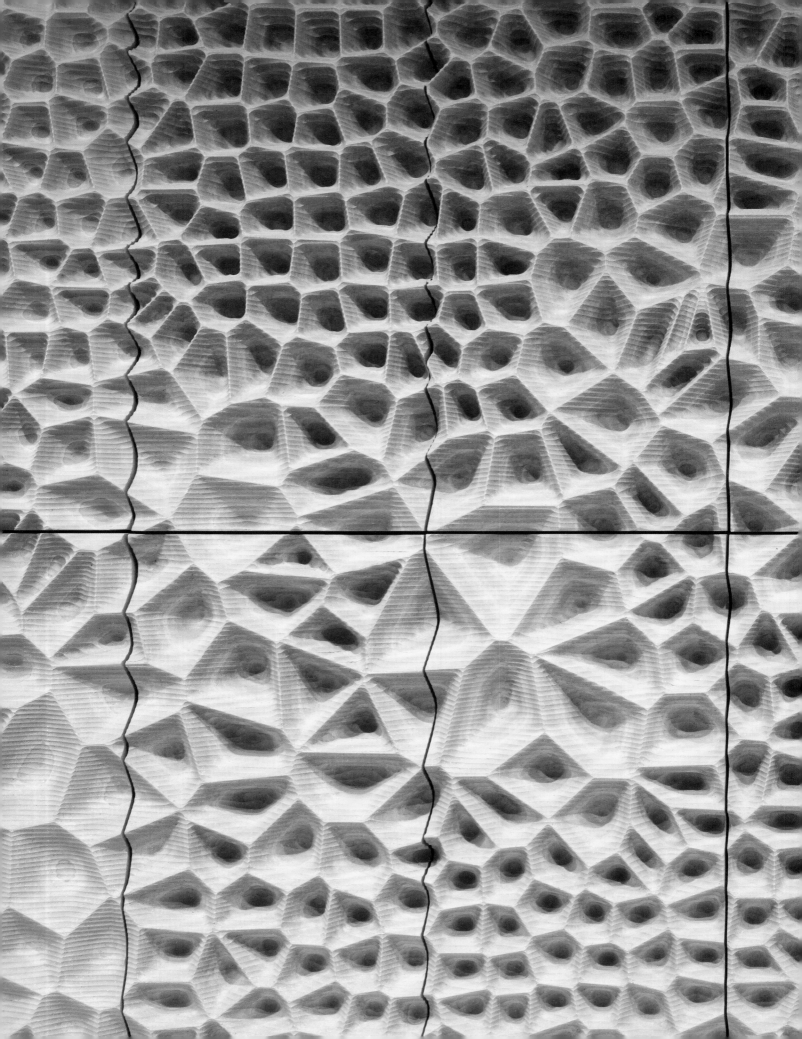

YASUHISA TOYOTA'S SEARCH FOR THE IDEAL CONCERT HALL

The Beatles or the Stones? Hamburger SV or FC St. Pauli? Star Wars or Star Trek? These classic questions of taste are easy to answer compared with the question of a concert hall's ideal form. A question made all the more difficult by the large number of factors involved, each of which can affect all the others.

For the Elbphilharmonie's Grand Hall, one thing was clear from the start: the new space should have a place among the world's ten best concert halls. The world's very best music venues include classics like the Wiener Musikverein or the Amsterdam Concertgebouw, modern classics like Hans Scharoun's Berliner Philharmonie, and of course contemporary eyecatchers and earcatchers like Frank Gehry's Walt Disney Concert Hall in Los Angeles, or the Lucerne Culture and Congress Centre (the 'KKL') by Jean Nouvel. Wherever you look—and listen—there are huge differences between spaces. But, in the end, concert-hall design always has to answer a fundamental question: shoebox or vineyard?

Auditoriums known as 'shoeboxes' have right angles, making it comparatively easy to calculate how sound waves will behave as they move from stage to audience. Many famous concert halls were built on this principle. Their characteristic sound environment has to be learned, by both musicians and audiences. And they also have a sociological aspect: within the hall, there are obvious better spots, and worse ones. The best, of course, are the boxes in the gallery, from where you can look down at and be looked up to, or the front-row seats, which include seeing and being seen in the price of the ticket. The 'vineyard' model is more democratic and more contemporary. These spaces tend to be flatter, with their audiences

Precision job: the 'white skin' consists of thousands of routed gypsum fibre panels which, depending on their position in the room, will reflect sound waves to enable an optimal acoustic experience. Every single panel is one of a kind.

YASUHISA TOYOTA
THE ACOUSTICIAN

Acoustics is the science of sound and its propagation. To create perfect acoustics not only requires an understanding of the laws of physics, but also a broad knowledge of building materials and their effect on the dispersion of sound within a space. The acoustician Yasuhisa Toyota, born in Japan, is a perfectionist in this field. He has created exceptional acoustics in concert halls on four continents, including the Walt Disney Concert Hall in Los Angeles. One of the goals of his work is to allow the audience to hear consistently well throughout the hall, 'regardless of whether someone is sitting in the first or the last row'. With the Elbphilharmonie, this admirer of Brahms has created a masterpiece. In planning the Grand Hall, Toyota constructed a model of the room in a scale of 1:10 and calculated the acoustics to perfection.

less segregated: this means a fundamentally different experience of the music. The more daringly architecture moves in these new directions, the more the stage itself moves to the centre of attention, and to the centre of the hall. No longer off to one side, it is transformed from a work area to a display area, to be seen and appreciated from all sides.

The Berliner Philharmonie is the classic example of this innovative concert hall design. The musicians on the Berlin stage are much more part of a community than their Viennese colleagues in the Musikverein. Perhaps most importantly, they can also hear each other much better. But this way of thinking and of building puts immense demands on architects and acousticians. They have to come up with made-to-measure solutions, which requires a wealth of ideas and lively creative impulses. During the building phase, anything altered for practical reasons has to fit perfectly with the aesthetic concept: without harmony, there is no Philharmonie.

The form of the Grand Hall was inspired by La Scala in Milan, with its tiered balconies, but also by good football-stadium design, which allows the crowd to sit almost directly at the edge of the pitch. The best example of modern stadium-design philosophy is another Herzog & de Meuron creation: the Allianz Arena in Munich, with its enormous web-like facade lit from within. 'We are searching for a more organic form with a certain compactness,' was how Jacques Herzog described his vision for the Elbphilharmonie. 'We want to develop a space which brings people very close to the musicians. The people should make the space.' In 2005, a consultation hearing with experts came up with a neat formulation: 'a hall without hierarchy'.

Yasuhisa Toyota, a Japanese acoustician and a lover of Brahms and Mozart, was allotted the task of giving the Elbphilharmonie's centrepiece a sound as unique and extraordinary as its exterior. He had a difficult job: he was responsible for the sound of an auditorium which had the orchestra right in the middle, but one where the audience—especially behind the orchestra—should never feel they are seeing better than they are hearing.

Over the course of his career, Toyota has set new global standards in acoustic design, creating halls like the Suntory Hall in Tokyo and the Danmarks Radio Koncerthuset in Copenhagen. He also worked in close collaboration with conductor Esa-Pekka Salonen in constructing a new home for the Los Angeles Philharmonic. The best indicator of Toyota's influence on the work of the architects—who had never previously built a concert hall—is the radical changes made to their original designs for the Grand Hall. The first version of the hall had balconies with more pronounced curves; the second was more angular, and with a larger number of levels. The most noticeable change of all was the addition of a large sound reflector above the stage, almost fifteen metres tall. This has roughly the same proportions as in Toyota's Los Angeles design, but otherwise comparisons are difficult, since every Toyota space is unique in its proportions and in the materials used.

The Grand Hall was designed for classical concerts in general and for orchestral performances in particular. The crucial factor in Toyota's fine-tuning of the space is how the wall surfaces cope with problematic echoes: this was the reason for the wave-shaped 'white skin', which reflects sound in several directions. One important indicator for sound quality is the speed of the echo back to the stage: in the Grand Hall, this measures about 2.2 seconds. This means the room falls into a good rule-of-thumb range—it should be between two and three seconds. But an echo in that range does not by any means guarantee that the hall will sound good. Moreover, 'good' acoustics always have an element of subjective impression. Toyota's work was made even more difficult by the demand that the space also be suitable for electronically amplified concerts, which require a shorter echo time.

In the summer of 2007, a warehouse in Hamburg's Veddel district was prepared to house a 1:10 model of the Elbphilharmonie. Toyota normally works by building a model on which colleagues then conduct minutely detailed digital experiments. The first stages of research on the architects' designs were done with a computer; but at a certain point, theory is no longer enough.

A specialist firm from south Germany built the wooden model of the original, complete with cables and sensors, weighing 4.5 tons, and 5 x 5 x 3.5 metres in size. To get inside the model, you used a hatch in the middle of the Grand Hall. And the interior looked exactly like the as-yet-unbuilt original. Except smaller, of course. The small human figures on their chairs wore felt clothing. Crucially, distributed around the model concert hall were miniature loudspeakers, producing different test sounds at 65 different locations around the space. But the engineers could not check it with the naked ear: the frequencies are too high for human hearing. It was not only the size of the room that was made in precise proportion to the original. The air, too, was a special mixture, with plenty of nitrogen on hand to lower the oxygen content from twenty per cent to just over five. The €200,000 that the model cost was a wise investment: anything left uncorrected at this stage could not be changed later at the real-life building site—or only at enormous additional cost.

After the four months of testing, the scale model of the Elbphilharmonie was moved to the HafenCity district, within sight of the original. Since October 2008, the model has been on display in a 32-ton glass-and-steel cube at the Magellan-Terrassen, a new public space in the HafenCity area. Artefacts of the construction phase are exhibited on the ground floor of the cube, while twenty headphones in the pavilion's exterior walls give a taster of the Elbphilharmonie's concert programme. The model itself is located on the upper floor, where it was the starting point for public tours of the construction site, the place where guests got their first look at the project. When tours were no longer possible, the city organized an alternative: the river launch Lütte Deern was rechristened the MS Elbphilharmonie, and from May 2015 on, it cruised around the building every Sunday.

The key factor was the absolute determination—expressed time and again by those involved with the project—that the Grand Hall would achieve the best sound possible in the available space. There are plenty of mediocre concert halls in the world, and they cost a lot less money. Toyota himself found an elegant phrase for his acoustic ambition. As he said at the mounting of the Grand Hall's 'white skin' in January 2014: 'Unfortunately, I do have to admit there is no "best seat in the house". But there are an awful lot of very good ones.'

GRAND HALL

GESAMT-KUNSTWERK BALANCING FUNCTIONALITY AND EFFECT

It is probable that the design of the Grand Hall would have been less radical had Jacques Herzog and Pierre de Meuron not been such big football fans. Think of the rousing feeling that you know and love from stadiums, where what you want more than anything is to see the whites of the players' eyes. Where proximity to the action is the reason that the moment feels so immediate and emotions run high. Where the air around you rings with thwacks and cracks and falls totally silent in the seconds before the penalty kick, and burns in the seconds afterwards. This was the exact feeling that Herzog and de Meuron wanted to recreate as the centrepiece of the Elbphilharmonie. A space that brings you so close to the collective adventure of music that you become a participant in it, where the notes suck you in and send you free-falling into the sublime. A place that can give just under 2,100 people sitting in their seats the feeling that they haven't missed a thing, no matter whether they are right up against the stage or seated in the very back row, 30 metres away from the emotional epicentre. The most important question here: how to keep firm control over unwanted sound? After all, it isn't as if this concert hall, which at 12,500 tons weighs as much as nearly two-dozen Airbus A380s, is part of a structure in which nothing happens except for music. On the contrary, it is part of an extremely complex piece of mixed-use architecture, fitted precisely between a hotel and private apartments. Even the greatest music lovers among the inhabitants of these nearby rooms would be inclined to complain if they were shaken from their beds by the thunderous blows from the finale of Mahler's Symphony No. 6! Or, at the other extreme, the annual Grand Arrival Parade that celebrates the anniversary of the Port of

The lobbies surrounding the Grand Hall present an absorbing backdrop, guiding concert-goers to the musical experience.

In many concert houses, foyers are merely paths to the concert—means to an end. On this point, the Elbphilharmonie clearly has more to offer. Its foyers were constructed to constantly offer new, changing vistas of the outside of the Grand Hall. In the 'Helmut and Hannelore Greve Foyer' on the 13th floor, a 20-metre-long bar greets concert guests. There are also four small bars and a VIP lounge. And artists have access to an additional bar in the backstage area.

The art of sound: in the Grand Hall, music will be the centre of attention. That won't be easy, however, given the competition from the space itself. Football stadiums, which aim to get viewers as close to the action on the field as possible, count among the architects' inspirations for the spatial experience here. Despite the giant dimensions of the concert hall, the farthest distance from the conductor is a mere 30 metres.

Game-changing: the reflector over the stage of the Grand Hall has a major impact on the quality of the sound.

Hamburg with more than 300 vessels: imagine, just as the audience in the Grand Hall settles into enjoying the quiet passages of a Schubert sonata, some enormous floating hotel of a cruise liner blows its horn outside. Or: in the Grand Hall, the sounds of Beethoven's Ninth with its grand choral finale roaring nearly unchecked through the walls and into the adjacent Recital Hall to interrupt a Bach cello suite. So that the necessary calm prevails in both directions, the Grand Hall is acoustically autonomous. It is encased in two shells; the 362 steel spring elements between them ensure that the inner and outer shells, although just centimetres apart, never touch. 'A concert hall is the instrument on which the orchestra plays,' Sir Simon Rattle once said. As long-time music director of the Berliner Philharmoniker, he knew exactly what he was talking about. Clothes make the man; performance spaces support and shape an orchestra. The more often it

plays in a particular hall, the more comfortable and at home it feels, the more impressive the result. Without its influential home designed by architect Hans Scharoun, the Berliner Philharmoniker of the 20th and 21st centuries would be as unthinkable as the orchestras that were shaped by the historic music spaces of Vienna, Boston and Amsterdam. It was the combination of the young Rattle and a brand-new concert hall that put the City of Birmingham Symphony Orchestra on the map internationally; Finnish conductor and composer Esa-Pekka Salonen achieved similar results with the Los Angeles Philharmonic, after moving into the fresh concert hall designed by Frank Gehry in 2003. A new concert hall is always more than a statement of cultural policy. It holds the promise of something different, something greater. The ambition of the Grand Hall and its dimensions is evident just by looking at the design sketches. The public areas start on the twelfth floor and end on the seventeenth. Measuring 40 metres on the north-south axis and 50 metres on the east-west axis, the Grand Hall takes up about a third of the floor space under the rippling glass waves. The stage is about 25 metres from the ceiling's highest point. Conventional halls place the orchestra at the edge of the space; the more an interior's design approaches the 'vineyard' style of seating, the closer the orchestra moves towards the centre. In the Elbphilharmonie, the conductor, placed at the very centre, is in a visual position of power at the heart of the concert.

The building's glass facade is not the only element that evolved over the course of its planning. The Grand Hall also experienced changes that altered its look and feel. In the first draft, the room was still fairly smooth in shape, its balconies blending into one another gradually, like flowing waves. The surfaces of the boxes and balconies were reminiscent of a layer cake. The tiered structure continued with pleasing regularity all the way up to the ceiling. The colour scheme as displayed in the computer rendering—bright oranges and yellows—gave the interior a gentle glow. This approach was modified in the spring of 2006. The number of seats behind the stage was reduced to 200. The 'white skin', a fascinating surface of gypsum fibre panels, which in reality is light grey, now became the design element that would make the most formative impression. One must look at the 'white skin' up close in order to understand and, quite literally, feel its uniqueness. It consists of about 11,000 individual elements, the production of which took more than a year. Almost 6,000 square metres sculpted with extreme precision. Exactly 999,987 sound grooves, the deepest of which measures several centimetres, the shallowest just a few millimetres. And each individual element is always separated from the next by exactly five millimetres.

The price originally calculated for this huge puzzle, whose individual pieces were temporarily stored on 2,000 pallets in a hangar in Billbrook, a quarter in the Hamburg-Mitte borough, was €3.5 million. In the end, the bill came to €15 million for 6,000 square metres weighing 226 tons. The planning for the whole affair lasted two years, the assembly took just as long. Each element is one of a kind, manufactured by the company Peuckert in Mehring, a town east of Munich. Some weigh up to 150 kilogrammes per square metre. Beginning in December 2013, they were mounted on a custom-made skeleton constructed of laser-welded steel structures. This

part of the construction site resembled a sci-fi set more than a classical-music venue. The construction could be considered another world premiere for the concert house. That the pieces of 'white skin' taken as a whole look so spectacular is a convenient side effect, because their actual task is much more important: to reflect the sound waves that originate from the stage so precisely that out of each unique physical element comes a distinctive sound. The skin's rippling surface is incidentally both an allusion to the Elbphilharmonie's location on the banks of the Elbe and a quotation of the shape of the building's wave-like roof with its eight indentations in the shape of partial spheres. When journalists were invited on 3 February 2016 to a presentation in the Grand Hall, Jacques Herzog surprised them by expressing the hope that the 'white skin' would in the future no longer be known by this name. It reminded him, he said, far more of something mineral, of a cave, of a sense of 'nurturing containment'. Herzog compared the shape of the hall to a tent, to stadiums, and to ancient amphitheatres. Culture Senator Barbara Kisseler was ready for the occasion with a cryptic Chinese proverb: 'Many years pass before one finds a treasure.' And Pierre de Meuron added with anticipation: 'The acoustics are working already.'

Among the numerous considerations that go into crafting good orchestral sound, reflection from above is extremely important. Sail-like elements, which can be more or less elaborately mounted beneath the ceiling of a concert hall, constitute a popular means to this end. If you want to make things particularly complicated, you can introduce movable elements, which can be adjusted according to need or taste. The huge undulating panels at the new Philharmonie de Paris by Jean Nouvel are a current example of this.

The approach taken in Hamburg is less playful, aimed instead systematically at a result: a cross between a giant showerhead and a mushroom hangs at a height of 15 metres above the stage. Weighing 30 tons, solid, anything but delicate, it is covered on its underside with 'white skin'. Firmly fixed, it is a sort of acoustic guardrail for the musicians who play beneath it. If it did not hang there, the music would fizzle out in the far corners of the space. It houses lighting and technical equipment and, as a special treat, a remote console for the four-manual organ, even more well-hidden than the actual instrument, which many visitors are unable to see at first glance.

When Yasuhisa Toyota visited the construction site in January 2014 to see the emergence of his vision with his own eyes

PHILIPP KLAIS
THE ORGAN BUILDER

'A concert hall without an organ is like a book without letters,' says Philipp Klais. Born in Bonn, Klais comes from a family of organ builders going back four generations. For 130 years his family business has set its stamp on the international field of organ construction like no other. Klais organs can be heard in Cologne Cathedral, in Beijing, in Buenos Aires—and in the Elbphilharmonie. 'Every organ is a unique instrument, designed specifically for its acoustic, architectural and cultural surroundings,' says Klais. An organ builder must tune the instrument's intonation to its cultural environment. He therefore has designed the instrument for Hamburg to have a north-German timbre.

A gigantic concert organ is hidden in this picture. 'A more modest version than this cannot be seen in any other concert hall in the world,' its builder says.

from atop the scaffolding high in the hall, he said, amused: 'It looks a bit like a limestone cave.' In the new draft, the grid of the balcony had been purged of all extras, becoming downright sparse. Only the bare essentials, no distraction from function, seemed now to be the motto. The dominant impression is now the audience itself. Listeners are not merely decorative; they also become anonymous elements of the architecture. After all, their presence affects the sound.

Although the room can seat approximately 2,100 people, it feels—compared with other halls and in spite of its powerful size—surprisingly compact. Not as intimate as a chamber-music hall, but also not oversized like the unfortunate concert hall known for its poor acoustics in the Gasteig, the cultural centre in Munich. The Berliner Philharmonie is noticeably flatter than the Elbphilharmonie; the Walt Disney Concert Hall in Los Angeles also gives the eye freer range. However, in the Hamburg concert hall, you are right in the middle of everything, and not a single seat feels too far removed from the action. Furthermore, looking down from the higher sections of the crag-like balconies onto the stage gives the whole experience an alpine feel—a geographically unusual sensation for Hamburg citizens accustomed to the flatness of the North German Plain.

To the right of the conductor's podium, fairly high up, a discreet curtain of metal tubes had been visible in former computerized renderings—a small portion of the spectacularly large organ hidden beneath the undulating skin of the room. The organ pipes are the tip of an iceberg composed of metal and high-tech innards, constructed by a company in Bonn known worldwide for its specialized work. This is not the first Hamburg organ designed by Philipp C. A. Klais and his staff. They were also involved in the renovation of the Lutheran main church of St. Michaelis. His credo: 'We don't sell a product, we sell sound.' A Klais organ cannot be ordered from a catalogue. Difficulties in realization are perceived, at most, as challenges. Klais's workshop never takes on more than four instruments at once; in this the boss is adamant.

Klais's customers are scattered all over the globe; he builds for brand-new concert halls as well as for centuries-old churches. And Klais makes the seemingly impossible possible. Because the Scottish estate of an investment banker was not otherwise accessible for the final assembly of a salon organ, Klais transported the individual pieces by helicopter. He once delivered a mobile organ by train to the Sultan of Oman. Klais is also specific when it comes to choice of materials. For the bellows, he uses kangaroo leather rather than sheep leather. The Bonn company cooks its glue according to a traditional family recipe. Spruce or oak are harvested only in the winter and only during a waning moon to avoid sap in the wood that can lead to infestation. The lumberyard is located behind the headquarters of the company, which was founded in 1882; the Klais family lives right next door.

Klais's custom-made piece for Hamburg is four storeys high, a whopper of an organ. It has 4,863 pipes, 65 registers and four manuals with mechanical playing action. It measures fourteen metres wide and about fourteen metres high. The smallest tin pipe is just eleven millimetres short, the largest wooden pipe ten metres long. The 'staircase' inside measures thirteen metres in height. Built-in fire and sprinkler system are included. There is a console in the gallery directly in front of the organ and an electric mobile console, which can be placed on the orchestra stage. A smaller choir organ is located in the stage area behind the choir. Organs in other halls hover majestically far away. Not this one. It is designed and built to be so transparent that you can pass by without seeing it. You can even look through the facade formed by its pipes to see inside. Organ builders hate fingerprints on their pipes. These ones, made of tin alloy, were given a special paint job to keep them from rusting, in spite of many fingerprints. Here, the queen of instruments has been installed and is staged with a sense of grassroots democracy not to be seen anywhere else. An instrument for everyone in a concert house for all.

'No other concert hall in the world has its organ integrated into the space as modestly as this,' says Klais. His opinion on the hoped-for acoustic character: 'Hamburg is characterized by a very clear, direct way of speaking.' It was his intention with the Elbphilharmonie organ to 'bring more nuance into the language. It can and should not ever enter into competition with the fascinating instruments of Hamburg's churches, but should be specifically focused on the requirements of a concert.' Thus, far from being an all-purpose instrument— a kind of Swiss-army knife of organs that can handle every repertoire from blistering avant-garde to old music—it is instead a custom-built organ, suitable above all for Romantic and contemporary music.

A private donor, the Hamburg-based industrialist Peter Möhrle, took care of the costs of the organ—about €2 million. This resolved an acute problem for the city at the time, but in

The vineyard-style slopes provide dramatic views of
the hall and orchestra stage.

Klais's industry, one is already used to thinking in terms of
much larger timespans: 'In contrast to Cologne Cathedral,
begun in 1248 and finished under pressure from Prussia in
1880, the Elbphilharmonie is in actuality a high-speed project,'
Klais commented with reference to the Elbphilharmonie's
planning and construction woes.

As is their wont, the designers Herzog & de Meuron paid
attention to every detail, including the seats in the Grand
Hall. Creating a seat for the Elbphilharmonie turned out to be
a cross-border project: designed in Basel and manufactured
by Poltrona Frau in northern Italy, the custom-made seats
were named after the international three-letter shorthand
for Hamburg airport: 'HAM'. The 'HAM' also cites the entire
building in its design: the grey pattern of the wool cover re-
calls the dots of the glass facade. And each 'HAM' is installed
over small vents on a fairly rough oak floor, in harmony
with the light roughness of the 'white skin'. 'Everything has
a certain directness,' says architect Ascan Mergenthaler,
describing the interior's philosophy. 'This isn't an architecture of concealment.' That is to say: everything in the room
should be in support of the action on the stage.

A classical 'shoebox hall' is spatially straightforward, with a
clearly defined top, bottom, front and rear. The many-
cornered, winding turbine of feelings that constitutes the
Elbphilharmonie makes things more complicated. Each angle
of entry offers a different perspective. The Grand Hall is not
merely a hall, but a Gesamtkunstwerk of function and effect,
reason and victory. 'Music is made for people who ask
questions,' conductor Teodor Currentzis once said. A concert
hall like this one is the ideal place to search for answers.

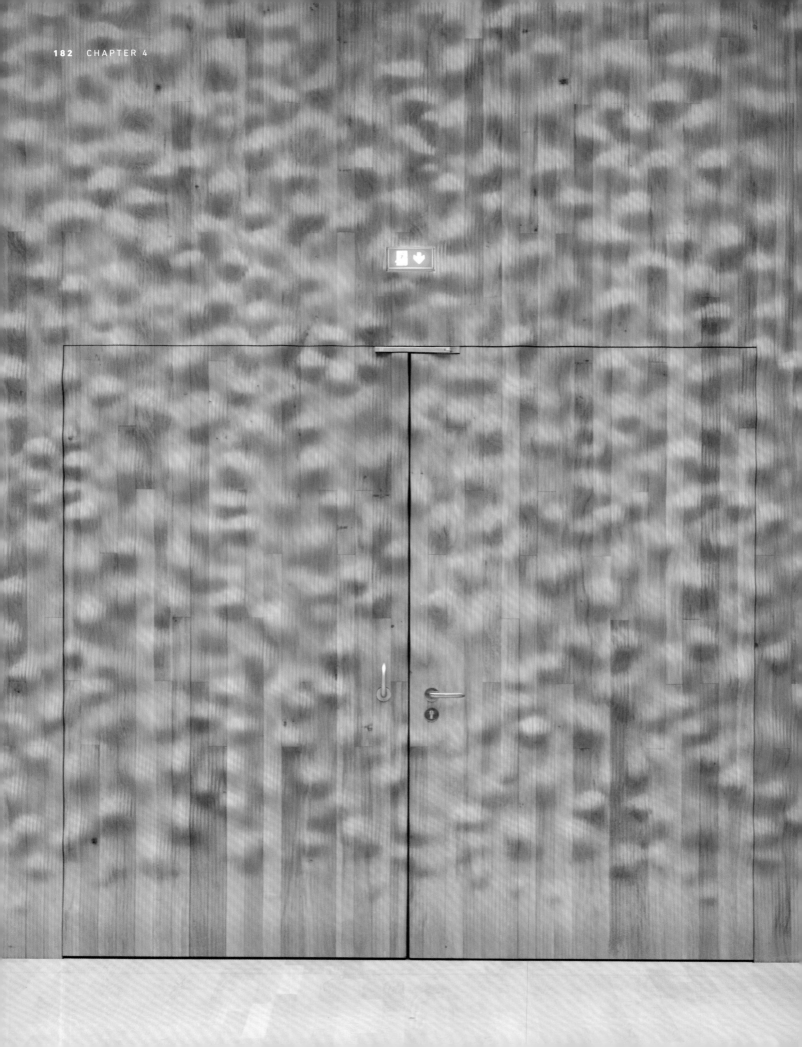

CHARACTER IS NEVER A QUESTION OF SIZE

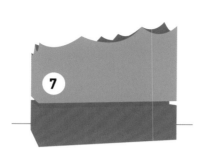

The Recital Hall is outfitted with wall panels that are similarly special, but with an entirely different design. These oak panels offer a fascinating contrast to the routed gypsum fibre panels in the Grand Hall.

Eight corners, four walls, a floor, a ceiling. The 'shoebox' model. It doesn't get more classic—and supposedly more 'conventional'—than this. But the Recital Hall is so much more than just a second space for anything too small or too acoustically specific for the Grand Hall, which at times can seem a bit 'Star Wars', just a little overwhelming. This second auditorium, also reached by a staircase leading from the Plaza, is a work of art in its own right. Like the Grand Hall, it was built to the highest possible standards, but with a completely different aesthetic. Even the stairs to the Recital Hall are designed to prepare visitors for its unique atmosphere. As visitors approach from the Plaza, each upward step takes them deeper into a different setting, into a very different mindset.

Like the Grand Hall, the Recital Hall is equipped with a double-layered exterior; it rests within its own soundproof concrete shell, buffered by 56 steel spring suspension elements. Thirty metres long and ten metres high, the hall covers 460 square metres. It can fit up to 572 seats, configurable in whatever way is best suited for the event, whether featuring soloists, chamber music or small ensembles. (By comparison: the Laeiszhalle's recital hall has 639 seats, all fixed in place.) The stage measures 90 to 172 square metres, with 18 elevating podiums to create stage effects. And its own backstage area, of course. But these are just dry facts and figures.

What will really turn this performance space into a treasured location, imbued with countless musical memories, is the astonishing resonance of its walls. 'Panelling' would be far too profane a term for their surface, not remotely doing justice to the landscape of French oak enclosing the sound-space in warm brown. Some 860 square metres of wall

Above: the lobby of the Recital Hall alludes to the panelling within.
Right: the technology of the room from an other perspective.

surface has been minutely indented with wave-shapes, thousands of miniscule peaks and troughs, with each wall panel individually created, its surface design a mixture of chance and careful calculation. A mountainous surface designed for sound waves, which spreads them through and around the hall, rather than echoing too directly between the long side walls. In theory, it sounds complicated. In practice, it sounds great.

Hanging from the ceiling are around two-hundred lamps, fitting discreetly into the overall design. As in a great sports car, the really interesting details here are those you don't notice at first glance. The ingenious ventilation, for example, which works so brilliantly that the audience is completely unaware of it. Or the telescopic seating, hidden away in the wall behind the last row of seats. This was made to measure in Austria, has seventeen different gradients, and comes with enough variations to suit any possible occasion.

In German, the Recital Hall goes by the name of 'Small Hall', which makes it seem somewhat less important than it actually is. Which just goes to show: character is never a question of size.

In the Kaistudios, only a few metres
removed from the concert halls, music
classes take place.

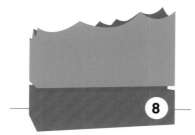

AN EDUCATION IN MUSIC

Something else very special is to be found on levels two and three, on the west side of the Kaispeicher: the Kaistudios. If upstairs is all about the classic triad of 'listening', 'seeing' and 'being seen', down here the focus is on musical education and communication. Practice makes a perfect listener. Hence the sloping ceilings, so the music will be reflected pleasantly. And extra-thick doors and lower benches set into wall-niches, with covers made from the same material as the Grand Hall's seats. Even in the toilets, smaller visitors have been taken into consideration.

These spaces are custom-made for the particular demands of music education. Seven different Kaistudios on two levels stand ready for curious visitors of every age, waiting to bring them into closer contact with music. During the day, this mostly means school groups, a practical application of the idea that the Elbphilharmonie is a building for everyone. First Mayor Olaf Scholz has put forward an ambitious and high-minded goal: that every Hamburg schoolchild should see the Grand Hall from the inside, at least once.

The original planning for this part of the building was very different. At first, the idea was to build a 'third auditorium' down in this part of the Kaispeicher, intended for children's concerts and educational events. In addition, the 'Klingendes Museum'—the hands-on 'Sound Museum', then based in the basement of the Laeiszhalle—would move into its own spaces in the building. And as such, the many construction delays turned out to be a blessing in disguise for this part of the project, as the plans were rethought on a much bigger scale. One room turned into seven. The largest room, Kaistudio 1, now covers 175 square metres, holding up to 170 people. It is equipped with all the necessary technology, and can accommodate a variety of seating arrangements and a small stage. If needs be, it can even take a concert grand piano. And, like the Grand Hall, this small space has daylight, streaming through two windows inserted into former loading hatches with views of the river's other bank.

Small but beautiful: Kaistudio 1 will be a 'training camp' for young visitors, preparing them for concerts in the Elbphilharmonie's larger concert halls.

Around the corner from the entrance, the architects have turned another loading hatch into a viewing balcony, with enough space for a bar, so older Kaistudio 1 visitors can have a drink.

The other six studios range from 30 to 65 square metres in size. A display case with instruments greets visitors as they step out of the lifts on the third floor and is a reminder of the 'Klingendes Museum' that will soon take up residency at the Elbphilharmonie. Inside, there are musical instruments to be tried out and demonstrated: these are stored in movable cases, easily moved from one room to the next. In total, there is capacity for several school classes to visit every day.

The Kaistudios' interior design is a sign of their close integration with the main functions of the building. The same lamps seen here are also to be found on the Plaza and in the Grand Hall; the florescent tubes here are also used elsewhere in the building. The spatial connections also cohere: you can take the lift from here and directly access the Plaza. From there, the auditoria are just a few steps away. There is no need for music education to stop where the concert area ends: rehearsals are to be accessible to visiting groups, who will thus experience the beauty of art—and the hard graft that goes into it—with their own ears. The intention of all this clever planning is clear, although sometimes not at first glance: at the Elbphilharmonie, everything is connected.

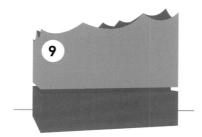

ROOM WITH A CONCERT

If a hotel guest in the bathtub of room 1902 could hear the start of a concert in the Grand Hall and follow what was on the programme that night, the Elbphilharmonie would have a real problem on its hands. Because of all the 244 rooms in the five-star-plus hotel, the Westin Hamburg, room 1902's bathroom sits directly above the concert hall. The nineteenth floor is special for other reasons too: not only does it feature the Eigner Suite, covering 160 square metres with views of the south-eastern glass verge, but also four two-storey maisonette suites with astonishing views of the port and the city, a real-life widescreen cinema. Two units look east towards HafenCity, one each facing north and south. The hotel's facilities extend beyond the glass tower above the Plaza. Down below, within the walls of the former Kaispeicher A, its facilities include, among others, a 1,300-square-metre spa and wellness centre, a 20-metre-long swimming pool, conference rooms, and a 170-seat restaurant. Some of the old loading bays have been turned into balconies for the restaurant and wellness areas. In total, the hotel—which belongs to the Arabella Hospitality Group—has 39 suites, more than any other hotel in Hamburg.

In coming up with the decor, interior designer Tassilo Bost drew inspiration from the building's surroundings and the riverside location. The foyer in front of the reception, accessible from the Plaza through a glass revolving door, has light-coloured oak cladding. The furniture in the rooms is understated. The interior design goes out of its way not to distract guests from the views of the city—which is why there are no pictures on the walls. Both in the bar and in the suites, softly rippling panels chime with the surface of the Elbe lapping against the brickwork below. And since the hotel bar is on the Plaza level—with an entirely glass frontage, of course—it is the ideal location for a drink after the last notes sound in the Grand Hall. The colour palette of the décor plays with shades of sand, aubergine, moss and copper; carpets

Open skies: one of the two-storey maisonette suites with a view of HafenCity's Sandtorhafen.

The floor-to-ceiling windows in the northeast corner of the Elbphilharmonie offer a widescreen panorama of the city.

and walls are greige; white and blue emphasize the hotel's position between river and sky. But it seems unlikely that a newly arrived guest will pay much immediate attention to the decor: they'll be too busy staring out of the floor-to-ceiling glass walls of their room or suite.

A twist of fate means two Austrians are the first occupants of the two top jobs in the Elbphilharmonie building. Christoph Lieben-Seutter, as general artistic director responsible for all artistic decisions, is originally from Vienna and he previously ran the Konzerthaus in that city. And on the hotel side, Dagmar Zechmann, also an Austrian, takes care of the overnight guests. Her previous positions include one at Vienna's legendary Hotel Imperial, directly beside the Wiener Musikverein, so she knows a thing or two about what makes artists tick.

During the crisis years of the building's construction, Christoph Lieben-Seutter was repeatedly, if unwillingly, given more time to plan and think about alternatives. But Dagmar Zechmann had far less preparation time for the launch of the hotel. For both of them, the first weekend in November 2016 is marked in red on the calendar: on the one hand, the Plaza will be opened to the public, on the other, the hotel opens for business, directly and without a 'soft launch' phase, when complex practical details might have been ironed out.

The logistical demands of a hotel like this are immense, especially since it is not based on ground level, but rather on top of—and to some extent inside of—the enormous base of Kaispeicher A. Other hotels can have their suppliers deliver goods whenever suits them. But here all appointments have to be carefully coordinated using online software, ensuring that the truck with fresh breakfast rolls or new bathrobes can make it to the southern delivery zone without causing a traffic jam in front of the building. And the trucks can't be too big, otherwise it's a tight fit in the narrow passage between the building and quay. And since the number of people allowed on the Plaza is limited, careful account has to be kept of comings and goings from the hotel. Just a few of the challenges to deal with, all to keep hotel guests in the eastern part of the building happy.

Left: the bar area with its bright spots, and hotel floor with elevators.
Above: a bathtub to soak in the view.

Harbour aroma: operable vents are incorporated into the glass facade. Above right: hotel rooms on higher storeys offer a view of the building's roof. Below right: the building's dot-design pulls one's view from inside to out.

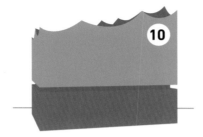

APARTMENTS

VERY CLOSE TO HEAVEN

As well as staying as a hotel guest in the Elbphilharmonie, it is also possible to live permanently in this building. Behind the western facade, between the eleventh and 26th floors, there are 44 apartments of the very highest quality, not a single one identical to any other. For the rest of the building, the key date on the horizon is 11 January 2017, when the first concert will take place in the Grand Hall. But the building and sale of apartments has a different schedule: by the second half of 2017, all apartments should be ready for occupation. The apartments are owned by Skyliving, a joint venture between construction firm Hochtief Infrastructure and real-estate company Quantum Immobilien. A contract with the city of Hamburg, signed in 2007, granted Skyliving the right to build and sell some forty apartments at its own expense. The apartments were never property of the city.

On the ground floor of the western facade there is a separate lobby for the owners and inhabitants of the apartments, with its own entrance and lifts. This is where the concierge is based, eager to fulfil every wish—possible and impossible alike—with speed and discretion. Parking is available in a private car park with 85 spaces.

Many of the floors of the apartment complex consist of just a single apartment; no floor has more than five. At the very top of the building, directly under the steeply pitched roof, four penthouse apartments have been tailor-made for the space. The smallest of the 44 apartments covers a manageable 120 square metres. The largest is 400 square metres. The 290-square-metre penthouse on the 25th and 26th floor boasts a ceiling height of up to seven metres, stretching over two floors at the building's highest peak.

On the 18th floor is a showcase apartment designed by British designer Kate Hume, including sauna, fitness area, and guest wing. There is marble and natural stone in the bathrooms, oak floors—the materials used are opulent. The colours in the living area have been chosen to go with the

Cinematic vista: the loggia of one of the private apartments offers a unique view of the HafenCity and Hamburg skyline.

Showcase apartment in the west wing
of the Elbphilharmonie, furnished by
the British designer Kate Hume.

panorama of sky, port and neighbouring rooftops: green, cobalt blue, and above all grey. There is much fashionable understatement.

It is hard to imagine how anyone could sit and work at a desk here, high over spectacular views of the Elbe. All the more so in May, when the boat ballet of Hamburg's annual Hafen-geburtstag—the 'port anniversary' festivities—takes place directly in front of the western balcony. You can imagine the apartment viewings: prospective buyers gazing dumb-founded at the views, downriver towards the ocean and the world. The apartments will be sold without furniture and without kitchens, giving free rein to their owners' creative preferences.

If an owner is away and is suddenly hit with the urge to close the curtains, a smartphone app allows full remote control. In five of the apartments, you have the pleasant choice between a loggia facing the river and one facing back towards the city. A dilemma, but hardly a problem. 'Living doesn't get more spectacular than this,' says one estate agent's brochure. It is no exaggeration: where else does a concert auditorium form part of a luxury development?

But there is one thing prohibited to the owners of these unique apartments. They are not permitted to make any alterations to the facade. Attaching objects of any kind is not allowed without written permission from the management. So no football flags hung from the balcony, no satellite dishes, no flower pots in the tuning forks of the glass facade. No flashing fairy lights for Christmas, no life-size Santas.

There is another rule, though, which makes up for this prohibition: the higher the apartment, the more breathtaking the panorama. On the 24th floor, you are so close to the sky that you glimpse another view, to the east, over the peak of the concert hall's sequined roof. The view, seen from any of the apartments' many windows, underlines just what a world-class rarity it is to live here. If you can afford it.

Above and left: eye to eye with
St. Michaelis: the showcase apartment
also features a fitness area.

A living room high above the roofs
of Hamburg with St. Michaelis
(Michel) offering the time.

Instead of photographs on your wall,
a genuine sunset: the city panorama
is a breathtaking spectacle.

The Kaiserspeicher was reminiscent of a Gothic cathedral. The time ball at the top of the tower fell every day at noon, ushering in the lunch break at the port. Kaispeicher A, which became the foundation of the Elbphilharmonie, was later erected in its place.

5

A Musical History
from the Oper am Gänsemarkt
to Kaispeicher A

Hamburg's famous houses of music.

The Laeiszhalle was a gift to the city.

Kaispeicher A was a landmark of the harbour.

The Hanseatic League, whores and a hallelujah!

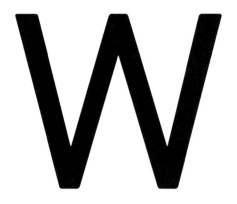

ere one to pick a date to mark the beginning of a public musical life in Hamburg, then the year 1660 would be a viable option, when the first public 'Collegium Musicum' concerts organized by organist Matthias Weckmann were held in the refectory of the cathedral. Or, alternatively, one might pick the year 1678, when the Oper am Gänsemarkt was inaugurated by Johann Theile's sacred opera, 'Adam und Eva oder Der erschaffene, gefallene und auffgerichtete Mensch'. The founding team consisted of an alderman, a lawyer and a church musician.

Designed by the Italian architect Girolamo Sartorio, it was the first civic opera house in Germany. With its elongated shape, the timber-frame building fulfilled its revolutionary purpose of making opera accessible to all. Challenging and sophisticated work intended for connoisseurs and aficionados found its place there, but so did simple entertainment, peppered with topical references to merchants and aldermen, to the morals (and moral failings) of middle-class society. Reinhard Keiser's two-part opera about the pirate Klaus Störtebeker was performed, as well as Georg Philipp Telemann's 'Emma und Eginhard', with Charlemagne as the father of the title character.

The young George Fredric Handel (then still called Händel) gained practical experience in the pit of this 'music-theatre' as second violin and harpsichordist. It was here that he wrote his first opera. In 1704, he nearly lost his life in the streets in front of the opera house during a legendary sword fight with his contemporary Johann Mattheson. Only a metal button kept his illustrious career from coming to a premature end. The curtain fell at the Oper am Gänsemarkt for the last time in 1738. Baroque opera, once so beloved, had grown unfashionable. And without further ado, the opera house was torn down. It was replaced by the Ackermann'sche Comödienhaus, which was bestowed with the pompous name of the Deutsches Nationaltheater in 1767. Gotthold Ephraim Lessing worked here as a dramaturge.

Musical life on the banks of the Elbe soon found another spot in which to flourish. On 14 January 1761, the Concertsaal auf dem Kamp was opened as an alternative to the Drillhaus of the Civic Guard on the Binnenalster (one of two artificial lakes formed within the city limits by the River Alster) and other similarly undistinguished establishments. National publications passed unanimously positive judgement on this new venue, Hamburg's first privately-run concert hall: 'The hall is well-designed, and the music resonates within it quite admirably, and 20 musicians can accomplish more there than perhaps 30 could elsewhere,' enthused the Musikalische Korrespondenz der Teutschen Filharmonischen Gesellschaft in 1792. Carl Philipp Emanuel Bach, Telemann's successor, gave many concerts there. This venue, however, would not last forever. First repurposed as a hospital, it became a barracks during the French occupation of Hamburg in 1813–14.

The Great Fire of Hamburg, which burned for three days in 1842, destroyed more than a quarter of the area then comprising the city; once the flames had been doused, the citizens spared no expense in rebuilding and treated themselves to a new venue by the Neuer Wall as well: the Tonhalle. In the next of many parallels to our present-day story, the Tonhalle received an impressive concert organ. The grand hall had over 1,500 seats and there was a beer hall in the basement. The acoustics were, however, merely average. For this reason, the Philharmonische Gesellschaft moved their concerts to the Apollosaal on the street named Großer Drehbahn in the northern part of the city. Not far away stood 'Sagebiels Etablissement', which contained seven rooms for all possible occasions, making it the largest facility of its kind in Germany.

Another venue was the Konzerthaus Ludwig on the Reeperbahn, built in 1889 and destroyed in the Second World War. Its features included a beer hall, a bowling alley and a winter garden complete with in-built waterfall. Gustav Mahler, chief conductor at the Stadt-Theater and known among Hamburg's orchestra musicians as being something of a quick-tempered pedant, conducted a five-movement version of his own Symphony No. 1 there in 1893, created especially for the occasion.

Over the course of the 19th century, a whole series of cultural buildings sprang up in Hamburg; none, however, added any sort of lasting sheen to the city's reputation. 'Public life in Hamburg doesn't allow for the nurturing of pure art [...], because here everything that isn't business is seen with eyes of pity or contempt,' the Wiener Allgemeine Musikzeitung said in 1845, by way of describing the prevailing mood. Unforgettable, too, was the scathing verdict of the poet Heinrich Heine: 'Whores aplenty, but no muses.'

The concerts of the Philharmonische Gesellschaft were influential for public life at the time. After a stint in the

1) The Oper am Gänsemarkt where Handel played in the pit in 1704 as a harpsichordist.
2) The Tonhalle at the Neuer Wall, which was equipped with the first great concert organ in Germany.
3) The Konzerthaus Ludwig at Millerntor, which was resplendent with a winter garden complete with a waterfall.
4) The Conventgarten, home to a hall known for its outstanding acoustics.

approx. 1.5 km away **16**

EDMUND-SIEMERS-ALLEE

LOMBARDSBRÜCKE

FELDSTRASSE

DREHBAHN **12** **13** DAMMTORSTR. GR. THEATERSTR. **15**

VALENTINSKAMP **11**

5

7
6

8 **9** FUHLENTWIETE

BUDAPESTER STRASSE

HOLSTENWALL

KAISER-WILHELM-STRASSE

10

14 JUNGFERNSTIEG

BINNENALSTE

BALLINDAM

3

18

NEUER WALL

HÜTTEN

4
REEPERBAHN

1

DOMSTRASSE

2

LUDWIG-ERHARD-STR.

ENGL. PLANKE

BÖHMKENSTRASSE

WILLY-BRANDT-STR

SANDTORKAI

AM KAISERKAI

NORDERELBE

20

FOLLOWING THE MUSIC

Hamburg is a city with a rich musical history. From the Conventgarten and the Oper am Gänsemarkt to Johannes Brahms's house and the Elbphilharmonie, the Staatsoper and the Laeiszhalle—a stroll through its streets that resonate with its musical past and present.

● Existing site

● Historic site

1 **MENDELSSOHN-MONUMENT** Ludwig-Erhard-Straße

2 **ST. MICHAELIS CHURCH (THE MICHEL)** Englische Planke 1

3 **BRAHMS MUSEUM** Peterstraße 39

4 **CONCERTHAUS LUDWIG** Millerntorplatz

5 **MUSIKBUNKER** Feldstraße 66

6 **JOHANNES-BRAHMS-PLATZ WITH MONUMENTS**

7 **LAEISZHALLE** Johannes-Brahms-Platz

8 **BRAHMS MONUMENT** Gängeviertel

9 **BIRTHPLACE OF JOHANNES BRAHMS** Speckstraße 60

10 **WÖRMERS CONVENTGARTEN** Fuhlentwiete 67

11 **KONZERTSAAL AUF DEM KAMP** Valentinskamp

12 **APOLLOSAAL** Drehbahn

13 **SAGEBIELS ETABLISSEMENT** Drehbahn

14 **OPER AM GÄNSEMARKT** Gänsemarkt

15 **HAMBURGISCHE STAATSOPER** Große Theaterstraße 25

16 **ROLF-LIEBERMANN-STUDIO** Oberstraße 120

17 **DRILLHAUS** Ferdinandstraße

18 **TONHALLE** Neuer Wall 50

19 **SAINT MARY'S CATHEDRAL** Domplatz

20 **ELBPHILHARMONIE** Platz der Deutschen Einheit 1

Opening concert of the Laeiszhalle with the Cäcilienverein, Hamburger Singakademie and the Verein der Hamburgischen Musikfreunde under the direction of Richard Barth, on 4 June 1908.

Apollo-Saal, they found a new home in the 'Wörmer'sche Konzertsaal' on Fuhlentwiete near the Binnenalster, opened in 1853. The venue was later redubbed the Conventgarten, a concert hall that, after additions were made in 1870–71, was said to have better acoustics than the Laeiszhalle, which opened nearly 40 years later. Yet the Conventgarten, too, is just a footnote to the city's musical history. In July 1943, it fell prey to aerial bombs. As the only large concert hall in Germany, the Laeiszhalle at least was spared.

The Laeiszhalle was realized by moneyed private individuals who nevertheless first had to convince the city's political overlords that their undertaking was a worthwhile one. The visionary idea of a music hall owned by shareholders had already fallen through once, in the 1860s. The intended location of the venue, the operations of which would have been financed by the purchase of shares, was the Moorweide, a large park in the southern part of the city. Comparable with the early days of the Elbphilharmonie, the city would only have needed to make the plot available and would have otherwise been uninvolved.

Spectacular designs had even been drawn up by Martin Haller, the architect who was later hired not only for the construction of Hamburg's City Hall, but also for the

Laeiszhalle. But after a long back-and-forth in the Bürgerschaft, the plans were quietly smothered by the city's bureaucrats. The Senate didn't want to feel responsible for supporting culture—a stance apparently not atypical for some politicians, then as now. From Haller, too, came the idea for a multi-purpose concert house that was to be built on the corner of Gänsemarkt and Neuer Jungfernstieg, in the best possible location: with two halls, restaurants and a hotel with a glass roof over the courtyard, which would have served as an entrance for both hotel guests and concert-goers—another Elbphilharmonie parallel.

But maybe these shattered dreams were precisely the thing that, some years later, paved the way for a different dream to succeed. In his will, the Hamburg ship-owner and Beethoven admirer Carl Heinrich Laeisz wrote that his company could transfer 1.2 million gold marks to the city, 'to build a worthy site for the playing and enjoyment of noble and serious music'. Using money to force the business people to reconsider proved a clever move. And when the wealthy Laeisz, who described himself ironically as 'musically impaired', shuffled off his mortal coil in March 1901, his widow, with equal parts of resolution and generosity, rounded the sum upwards. Two million gold marks for a fine new concert hall that from now on (it was hoped) would give this metropolis of trade, prone to self-importance, top billing in the programme of cultural treasures—the next parallel to the Elbphilharmonie.

'Hamburg has fallen considerably behind, not only in comparison with other major cities, but even with some smaller modern cities,' reported a study addressing the question of whether a new concert house was even necessary. 'Our city lacks monumental structures.' In this context, certain comments by architect Martin Haller remained unquestionably relevant: 'No one can deny that the beauty of a city or the sum necessary to accomplish it are important factors, not quantifiable through numbers alone, for the flourishing of that city.' Laeisz's widow expected two things from the city: no resistance, and a suitably located plot of land. The rest, she gave assurance, could be left to her. She hired architects Martin Haller and Emil Meerwein to design the neo-Baroque brick showpiece for her, which in its form cited Hamburg's St. Michaelis Church. The Leipzig Gewandhaus, with 1,524 seats, served as inspiration and reference. In December 1902, the Bürgerschaft decided to allocate 5,000 square metres on

Holstenplatz to build this concert hall 'for musical events of most distinguished style'. The 639-seat Recital Hall (which has since been refurbished in the style of the 1950s) as well as a 150-seat rehearsal room in the basement were included in the contractually agreed-on construction plan, in addition to the Grand Hall that seats 2,025 audience members.

On 4 June 1908, after four years of construction, everything was in place. The opening concert boasted a varied and representative mixture: a Bach passacaglia to show off the organ, Handel's Hallelujah Chorus from the 'Messiah', 'Fest-und Gedenksprüche' by Johannes Brahms (the 'honorary citizen' of Hamburg, born just around the corner) and Beethoven's Symphony No. 5, played by the Philharmoniker. If you're going to set about doing something, then you might as well do it right. Hamburg had put Germany's largest concert hall to work, and had orchestrated everything with appropriate pride and assurance. And, after wild rumours had circulated about the hall's aural features, the Hamburgische Correspondent, the city's respected daily, gave the all-clear: 'The acoustics can be accurately described as unobjectionable. It's no different with these concert halls than it is with a violin. They want to be broken in.'

Over time, the Laeiszhalle has become known and cherished as one of the finest venues in Europe, acoustically speaking. Vladimir Horowitz placed the first stone in the foundation of his career as a pianist here in 1926, and it was also home to his final German concert in 1987. Maria Callas sang here. Every major orchestra, every important conductor and virtuoso has performed on this stage. Rock, pop and jazz concerts have taken place here too, standing in odd contrast to the dignified hall, with its ornate and historic design. Over the decades, audiences got used to the Laeiszhalle as a stage for this and that.

When in 1997 the city of Hamburg held a festival in honour of the 100th anniversary of the death of Johannes Brahms, the former Karl-Muck-Platz (named after a conductor who had never made a secret of his sympathy for the Nazis) was renamed Johannes-Brahms-Platz. In 2005, three years before its 100th birthday, the concert house, which had also become known as the Musikhalle, was officially christened the 'Laeiszhalle' in a very belated 'adult baptism'. Since then, this name has served as a memorial to its well-meaning and resolute benefactors. They had shown the political sphere exactly how influential a passion for culture could be.

Sophie Christine Laeisz and her husband, ship-owner Carl Heinrich Laeisz. Without their commitment and their capital, the Laeiszhalle would never have been built.

Hamburg port and jetties in 1931: the Kaiserspeicher, with its distinctive tower, can be seen at the tip of the pier known as the Kaiserkai.

IT WAS THERE, ON THE BANKS OF THE GREAT RIVER, AT THE GATEWAY TO THE WORLD, THAT THE MONEY THAT HAD MADE THE CITY BIG AND STRONG WAS EARNED.

IN THE MIDDLE OF THE CITY, RIGHT ON THE LINE DRAWN THROUGH IT BY THE ELBE, NOBODY GAVE TWO CENTS ABOUT THE VALUE OF CULTURE.

For it was there, on the banks of the great river, at the gateway to the world, that the money that had made the city big and strong was earned. The buildings there, although magnificently executed, were not exactly storehouses for the emotions. They were spaces for offices and tradespeople and wares from all over the world. One of the most striking of its kind was the Kaiserspeicher at the westernmost tip of Grasbrook, an island between the northern and southern branches of the Elbe. In operation since 1875, it had cost 1.5 million marks to build. When, a few years after the end of the Franco-German War, director of hydraulic engineering Johannes Dalmann rammed the building's bulky, downstream-facing facade into the Hamburg landscape, he created a mercantile symbol of the city's soul and sensibility in the boom years after German unification. The Speicherstadt, the world's largest contiguous warehouse complex, was later modelled on its example. The Kaiserspeicher was a specimen reminiscent of a Gothic cathedral. Ships could approach it directly to load or unload their cargo.

Shaped like a giant isosceles triangle, its measurements were massive: each side a hundred metres in length, six floors high, 19,000 square metres of space and a courtyard with room for three sets of freight tracks. The boiler chimney was cloaked with a decorative tower; atop it, a time ball was drawn slowly upward beginning at 11.50 am each morning. Its fall, precisely at noon, signalled lunch break. The time ball also enabled navigators aboard ships offshore to verify the setting of their chronometers.

For anything coming upriver towards the city, the Kaiserspeicher acted as a kind of business card for Hamburg, moulded out of brick. Just behind it, the Speicherstadt with its facades like mediaeval castles stretched into the free harbour zone. Unsurprisingly, the port of Hamburg was a major target for bombers in the Second World War. After its end, only half of the Speicherstadt was left standing; of the Kaiserspeicher, little more than the tower with its time ball remained. Perhaps it could have been saved and reconstructed, but instead it was demolished in 1963.

The contract for the construction of Kaispeicher A went to the Hamburg architect Werner Kallmorgen. He envisioned a flat, unembellished, functional building that had almost no windows. His design was a block of brick, its four sides each a different length, coming nearly to a point at its westward end and broad and wide on its eastern side. Reduced in ascetic and brutal fashion to the bare necessities, it still possessed artful details such as fold-out hatches and derricks on the southern flank. Not so much a jewel of architecture in the classical sense, rather an operational tool.

Opting for this architect and his brand was simply logical. He came from a distinguished family of Hamburg architects and boasted an impressive portfolio. Werner Kallmorgen was also responsible for the renovation of the Speicherstadt area. Yet the concept was not blessed with good fortune. The Kaispeicher that went into operation in 1966 had been planned according to the needs of the time. Intended as a warehouse for general cargo, it measured 30,000 square metres—a floor with no courtyard. Plenty of space, but only in theory. For the days of general cargo were coming to an end; the container was about to become the unit by which all things were measured. Two years after the opening of the Kaispeicher, the first container ship docked in Hamburg—and changed everything. The new building, so recently still radical and visionary, became a relic of yesteryear occupying highly desirable real estate in the heart of the port.

The turning point came in the late 1990s with First Mayor Henning Voscherau's idea for a comprehensive transformation. HafenCity, the largest inner-city urban development project in Europe, was on its way. It was a time to dream big. The internet had claimed its place; the dot-com bubble was growing, and with it the idea of replacing the unsightly brick building—now little more than an aging piece of junk—with something trendy, something new.

The Kaiserspeicher tower was the landmark of Hamburg's port. It survived the Second World War but, rather than being saved, it was demolished in April 1963. Kaispeicher A was built in its place. But when the end of the 1960s brought with it the end of general cargo in the freight business, the unadorned building was no longer useful as a warehouse for barrels and crates, pallets and bags.

THOMAS HENGELBROCK
PRINCIPAL CONDUCTOR OF THE NDR ELBPHILHARMONIE ORCHESTER

In the first phase of his career, Thomas Hengelbrock was primarily associated with the topic of 'historical performance practice'. Born in Wilhelmshaven, Hengelbrock played violin in Nikolaus Harnoncourt's Concentus Musicus in Vienna, and founded the Balthasar-Neumann Choir and the eponymous Ensemble. In 2011 the internationally acclaimed opera director joined the NDR as Christoph von Dohnányi's successor. The principal conductor of the Elbphilharmonie's resident orchestra has used the waiting period before the opening concert well, directing a repertoire in Hamburg ranging from the Baroque to the Modern to promote himself and his orchestra as widely as possible.

River of Music

A new name, a new building, big plans—
for the NDR Elbphilharmonie Orchester.

Great conductors and composers shaped the
musical life between the Elbe and the Alster.

This is the sweet sound of Hamburg's musical history.

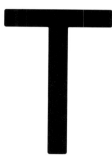

That thing about 'musical aroma' is actually really simple. Once you get beyond playing the right notes at the right time, any orchestra—from small-town amateurs to world-class ensembles—can only sound as good as its home auditorium allows. So if, after decades, an orchestra moves into a new concert hall, away from its native sonic territory, the space every musician knows like their own living room, the change is like installing a new operating system on a computer. After the re-boot, everything still functions, you can still work reasonably well, but all the details are somehow unfamiliar. That's how it will be with the Elbphilharmonie too. The sonic balance of the instruments in concert, the blind trust in the sensitive symbiosis of orchestra and concert hall, the delicate passage from mediocre to magnificent—all that takes time, patience and close attention.

So it was all the more crucial to give the NDR Orchester enough time to acclimatize. In April 2016, the directors of the radio orchestra presented their ideas and line-up for its first season in the new building. On that day, the orchestra also got its new name: no longer the NDR Sinfonieorchester, it became the NDR Elbphilharmonie Orchester. The name sends a clear message—and the acronym NEO also has a certain PR charm. There are plenty of examples of the publicity value for a city having an orchestra linked closely to its home venue—think of the Berlin Philharmonic, the Leipzig Gewandhaus Orchester, or the Royal Concertgebouw Orchestra in Amsterdam.

When, in 2005, NDR signed a contract with the city of Hamburg, making its ensemble the Elbphilharmonie's orchestra-in-residence, everyone thought it would be only four years to opening night. But by the time the doors open in January 2017, twelve years will have gone by.

Thomas Hengelbrock, born up the road in Wilhelmshaven, has been the project's figurehead and style guru, the non-authoritarian maestro at the heart of creative efforts. Previously a violinist in Nikolaus Harnoncourt's Concentus Musicus in Vienna, he came to Hamburg in 2011 as successor to Christoph von Dohnányi. He is a specialist in historical performance practice, with an extraordinary feel for the intentions and idiosyncrasies of composers and their music. Hengelbrock used the building's unexpectedly long lead-in time to thoroughly prepare the orchestra for the challenges they will face. For decades, the orchestra played its subscription concerts in the main hall of the Laeiszhalle.

Bright prospects: for the NDR Elbphilharmonie Orchester, the move to the new concert hall is the start of a new era. From left: Yihua Jin-Mengel, Bernhard Läubin and Andreas Grünkorn.

Three conductors have left a particularly strong impression on the NDR Orchester. Hans Schmidt-Isserstedt was asked to found it by the British occupying forces, then stayed for 26 years. The perfectionist Christoph von Dohnányi set the tone from 2004 to 2011. His successor Thomas Hengelbrock has prepared the orchestra for the move to the Elbphilharmonie.

Now, for its first season in its new Elbphilharmonie home, the orchestra will increase the number of its concerts by about a third, to a total of 125. In the opening season, about one third of all concerts in the Grand Hall of the Elbphilharmonie will be NDR performances. In addition, looking to lure in new audiences, it has developed a one-hour concert format for Sunday afternoons. There will also be 'late night' concerts, with a classical orchestra in one half and a contemporary pop act in the other, as well as open rehearsals, intended to give the audience a glimpse of the work done behind the scenes.

From the very beginning, NDR was at pains to emphasize how seriously it took the task of playing first violin to the city. But, in fact, this orchestra is not nearly as 'municipal' as the Philharmonische Staatsorchester, which is directly subsidized by the city government. By contrast, NDR finances its musical ensembles from the annual fees paid by all users of radio and television: it receives no money directly from state taxes. But even without government money, over the course of its history the orchestra has become a crucial part of Hamburg's musical landscape.

The history of the NDR Orchester began in the rubble and ashes of the city directly after the Second World War. It is inextricably linked with a man who was determined to make a great artwork out of nothing—**Hans Schmidt-Isserstedt**, its founding conductor.

But we should be clear: Schmidt-Isserstedt was far more than just a conductor. British officers tasked the former general musical director of Berlin's Deutsche Oper with putting together a radio orchestra for North-West German Radio (NWDR), using a temporary base in a farmyard not far from the city. Many of those he recruited were members of the Berliner Philharmoniker. He found musicians in prison camps, then held rehearsals in farmyards and guesthouses. 'Schmisserstedt' stayed 26 years on the job, his public persona gradually merging with the orchestra he had created. But this was not a conductor who was fond of burning calories on the podium. He always wanted to be an unobtrusive Kapellmeister rather than a grandiose podium diva. He kept modestly but doggedly to his motto: 'A conductor who sweats is not a conductor'.

He died just two years after retiring, the founding father to whom the NDR Orchester owed so much. After spells under the leadership of Israeli conductor Moshe Atzmon and then under Klaus Tennstedt, **Günter Wand** was the next iconic conductor to take charge. The Gürzenich Orchester in Cologne had actually made Wand take early retirement some years earlier, meaning that when he took up office in Hamburg in 1982, he was already 70 years old, just a year younger than Schmidt-Isserstedt when he left the orchestra. In 1987, with mutual admiration blooming on either side, Wand was named honorary conductor for life.

Wand was a phenomenon. The older he got, and the more he reduced his repertoire to a few key works, the greater the admiration from audience, orchestra and critics. Nothing disturbed his stoic, hard-working approach to rehearsals.

The Wand era lasted almost a decade, and it is still present and audible in the orchestra's DNA, especially when symphonies by Bruckner, Brahms or Beethoven are in the programme. With his sparse gestures, Wand literally brought time to a standstill.

After John Eliot Gardiner, Herbert Blomstedt and Christoph Eschenbach, in 2004 **Christoph von Dohnányi** made a comeback to Hamburg, the city where he once had the Staatsoper under his baton at the same time that his brother, Klaus von Dohnányi, commanded the Senate as the city's First Mayor. In the early phase of the Elbphilharmonie, the experienced Dohnányi repeatedly made provision for his successor's working conditions, offering valuable suggestions on practical questions. For example, Dohnányi is said to have influenced the placement of the stage in the Grand Hall; he also had an impact on the careful design of the backstage areas.

But Christoph von Dohnányi really earned his honoured place in the history of the Elbphilharmonie project with his appearance before a City Hall hearing. Members of the Bürgerschaft wanted to hear whether Hamburg actually needed a grand new concert house in the first place, and if so, why. Dohnányi coolly brushed off the parliamentarians' misgivings with a cultured, worldly counter-question: 'Well, was there a need for Beethoven's Ninth, or for Coca-Cola?'

FROM THE BAROQUE TO THE BEATLES

John Lennon once famously said: 'I was born in Liverpool, but grew up in Hamburg.' It is something that **Georg Philipp Telemann** could have said, a few centuries before—with the only difference being that he hadn't travelled quite as far. Unlike The Beatles on the Reeperbahn, the Baroque composer was no novice when he arrived in Hamburg in 1721 from the city of Magdeburg, a couple of hundred kilometres upriver. He certainly had a Lennon-sized ego and the ambition to go with it. In that year, Telemann stepped into a position with enormous prestige, becoming 'Director Musices' of Hamburg's five main churches, as well as cantor at the Johanneum. From then until his death 46 years later, he used the prominent appointments to garner fame and fortune. With Telemann calling the city home, Hamburg was the envy of the European music world.

His many responsibilities spurred Telemann into a life of prolific production. He delivered pieces for political occasions as well as for his own concert performances, and for the opera. Telemann composed more than twice as much music as Johann Sebastian Bach and Georg Friedrich Händel put together. More than 3,600 works flowed from his extraordinarily productive musical pen—around 50 operas and oratorios, 46 masses, psalms and Passions, 1,400 church cantatas, 70 secular cantatas and 40 songs, odes and canons, as well as 'captain's music' written for the annual banquets of the local militia. Add to that around 1,000 orchestral suites and more than 100 solo concertos for instruments including chamber, piano and organ music. No wonder later generations relegated him to the status of a 'wrote-too-much': no one could believe one musician could be that productive, and still that great.

Telemann's death, on 25 June 1767, at the age of 86, marked the end of an era. 'How many years would German music have

GREAT HISTORICAL FIGURES
are no rarity in Hamburg's musical history. Some world-famous composers were born here, others came here to build their careers. Over time, they formed a classical ensemble of melodious—and famous—names.

REINHARD KEISER
1674–1739
The Baroque opera composer put Hamburg at the heart of German opera culture.

GEORG PHILIPP TELEMANN 1681–1767
'Director Musices' for 46 years. In his lifetime, was admired like no other musical figure.

JOHANN MATTHESON
1681–1764
Baroque multi-talent: composer, conductor, musician and patron.

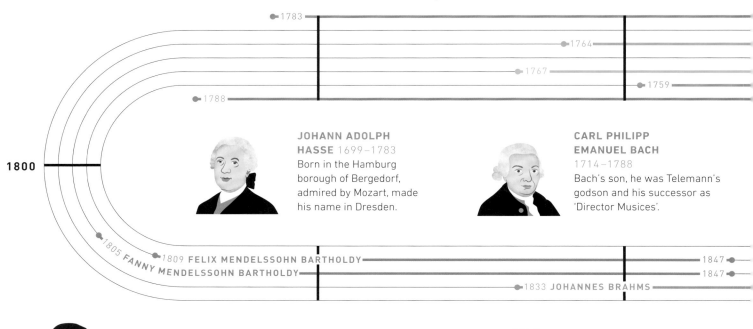

- 1783
- 1764
- 1767
- 1759
- 1788

1800

JOHANN ADOLPH HASSE 1699–1783
Born in the Hamburg borough of Bergedorf, admired by Mozart, made his name in Dresden.

CARL PHILIPP EMANUEL BACH
1714–1788
Bach's son, he was Telemann's godson and his successor as 'Director Musices'.

1805 FANNY MENDELSSOHN BARTHOLDY

1809 FELIX MENDELSSOHN BARTHOLDY — 1847

— 1847

1833 JOHANNES BRAHMS

GUSTAV MAHLER
1860–1911
Equally admired and hated as a Hamburg opera conductor, he eventually left for Vienna.

PAUL DESSAU
1894–1979
Fled from the Nazis into American exile, worked with Brecht, made a career in East Germany.

HANS SCHMIDT-ISSERSTEDT 1900–1973
The founder of the NDR Orchester served 26 years in charge. A legend on the podium.

- 1980
- 1996
- 1999
- 1996
- 1979
- 1973

2000

- 2002
- 2006

GÜNTER WAND
1912–2002
At the age of 70, he was appointed conductor of the NDR Sinfonieorchester.

GYÖRGY LIGETI
1923–2006
Already world-famous when he composed and taught in Hamburg.

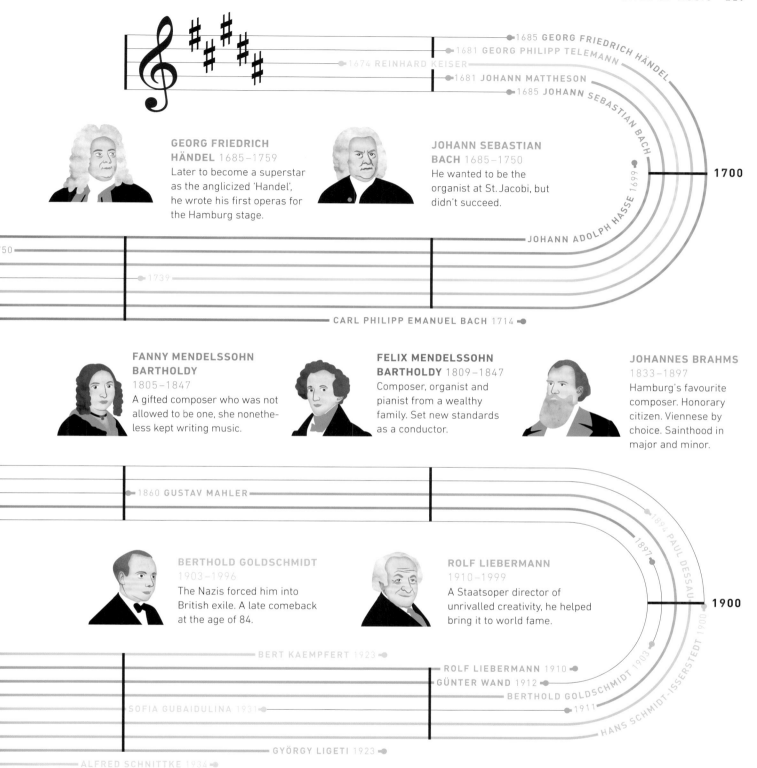

- 1685 **GEORG FRIEDRICH HÄNDEL**
- 1681 **GEORG PHILIPP TELEMANN**
- 1674 REINHARD KEISER
- 1681 **JOHANN MATTHESON**
- 1685 **JOHANN SEBASTIAN BACH**

JOHANN ADOLPH HASSE 1699

1700

GEORG FRIEDRICH HÄNDEL 1685–1759
Later to become a superstar as the anglicized 'Handel', he wrote his first operas for the Hamburg stage.

JOHANN SEBASTIAN BACH 1685–1750
He wanted to be the organist at St. Jacobi, but didn't succeed.

'50

1739

CARL PHILIPP EMANUEL BACH 1714

FANNY MENDELSSOHN BARTHOLDY 1805–1847
A gifted composer who was not allowed to be one, she nonetheless kept writing music.

FELIX MENDELSSOHN BARTHOLDY 1809–1847
Composer, organist and pianist from a wealthy family. Set new standards as a conductor.

JOHANNES BRAHMS 1833–1897
Hamburg's favourite composer. Honorary citizen. Viennese by choice. Sainthood in major and minor.

1860 GUSTAV MAHLER

1894, PAUL DESSAU

1897

BERTHOLD GOLDSCHMIDT 1903–1996
The Nazis forced him into British exile. A late comeback at the age of 84.

ROLF LIEBERMANN 1910–1999
A Staatsoper director of unrivalled creativity, he helped bring it to world fame.

1900

BERT KAEMPFERT 1923

ROLF LIEBERMANN 1910

GÜNTER WAND 1912

BERTHOLD GOLDSCHMIDT

SOFIA GUBAIDULINA 1931

1911

HANS SCHMIDT-ISSERSTEDT 1900

1903

GYÖRGY LIGETI 1923

ALFRED SCHNITTKE 1934

BERT KAEMPFERT 1923–1980
Gave The Beatles their first record deal, composed 'Strangers in the Night' for Sinatra.

SOFIA GUBAIDULINA 1931
World-class Russian composer, who made her home within earshot of Hamburg.

ALFRED SCHNITTKE 1934–1998
A twentieth-century classic, he also wrote ballet music for John Neumeier.

remained wretched and miserable, had no Telemann appeared to take music out of the darkness through his divine genius and great industry?' asked one obituary of the city's resident star composer. Telemann was buried in the centre of Hamburg, in the cemetery of the Gelehrtenschule des Johanneums, founded in 1529. Where the cemetery once stood is today the location of Hamburg City Hall: only a modest memorial plaque by its main entrance bears witness to Telemann and his extraordinary significance for this city.

More fertile ground for a stroll through Hamburg's musical history can be found in the Composers' Quarter in Peterstraße, where Telemann's life and work are richly honoured, alongside the achievements of his godson and successor **Carl Philipp Emanuel Bach**. Although in his own lifetime C.P.E. Bach was considerably more popular than his father Johann Sebastian Bach, over the years, the son receded from the consciousness of music lovers. In much the same way, **Johann Adolph Hasse** has today fallen into comparative obscurity. The opera composer, who was born in Bergedorf, then an independent town, now a suburb in the east of Hamburg, made his career in Dresden and Vienna before eventually dying in Venice. Carl Philipp Emanuel Bach was buried here in Hamburg; his grave is in the crypt of St. Michaelis.

The next truly great musical Hamburger had a sibling whose significance remains underestimated. **Felix Mendelssohn Bartholdy** and his sister **Fanny** were both born in Hamburg, children of a wealthy, art-minded banking family. Felix's talent was encouraged from early on; he quickly established himself as a composer and conductor with the sensational success of his music for 'A Midsummer Night's Dream'. But Fanny's talent remained permanently overshadowed by her brother. Their childhood home, located opposite St. Michaelis, does not survive, but a nearby memorial commemorates the siblings. Their respective musical styles may be some distance apart, but on the map at least, Mendelssohn and **Johannes Brahms** were near-neighbours. Brahms was born just a few streets away from the Mendelssohn household, but grew up in the proletarian Gängeviertel district, in a quite different social class. His father, himself a musician, was a determined supporter of his child's talent. But although Brahms spent almost half his life in Hamburg, his greatest successes came elsewhere. He failed to obtain a series of interesting jobs in the city—choir director of the Singakademie, for example—and some of his compositions went over badly with Hamburg audiences. A classic case of artist's bad luck. But his Viennese career went all the better for these setbacks, although Brahms, underneath his rough exterior, was often consumed by homesickness in the Austrian capital.

In 1889, Brahms was named an honorary citizen of Hamburg—the honour came late in life, but was well-deserved. Brahms was the first artist to be recognized in this way: the two recipients before him were Otto von Bismarck and Helmuth von Moltke, a politician and a military man, the two architects of the German Empire. When Brahms died in Vienna in 1897, the Hamburg Senate ordered flags in the city to be flown at half-mast, in honour of the gruff late Romantic. In the Brahms Foyer of the Laeiszhalle, he is commemorated with Max Klinger's great marble statue; on the square in front of the concert hall there are two separate monuments. Even today, a Brahms symphony on the programme is guaranteed to sell out fast.

Gustav Mahler's six years in Hamburg, where he was 'first music director' of the Stadt-Theater on Dammtorstraße, cannot exactly be characterized as peaceful. Gustav Mahler thundered wildly through his orchestral duties, looking to gain as much experience as possible with the repertoire, and he fought with his colleagues on every possible occasion.

The Hamburg institution through which Mahler stormed was above all a springboard for distant shores. He undoubtedly felt called to higher things and he proceeded to take the first opportunity to escape, making a beeline for the Vienna State Opera. However, his Hamburg years saw the composition of several important early works. At the funeral of Hans von Bülow, a conductor colleague he much admired, he heard a choral piece based on the poet Klopstock's 'Auferstehen wirst Du, mein Staub, nach kurzer Ruh', and had the crucial idea for the finale of his Second Symphony, dubbed the 'Resurrection Symphony' for this reason.

In January 1897 Mahler handed his resignation to the theatre's director Bernhard Pollini, a man he despised. In February of that year, Mahler, although Jewish, converted to Catholicism—a career-minded decision, essential for the Vienna job. Two months later, he left the city. When he died in Vienna in 1911, one Hamburg newspaper declared in its obituary: 'As a conductor, Mahler was head and shoulders above all others.' We are all clever with hindsight. Alongside the Mendelssohn Bartholdy siblings, Mahler is soon to be honoured by an extension of the Composers' Quarter in Peterstraße.

The golden age of Hamburg opera, ushered in by Mahler in the late nineteenth century, lasted only a few years. But the next great epoch, in the second half of the twentieth, lasted almost two decades. The man responsible was a visionary Swiss director named **Rolf Liebermann**. Before his appointment to run the Staatsoper, he had never been in charge of an opera house, and had no particular great plans at the time of his application. But Liebermann, the great-nephew of painter Max Liebermann, had done outstanding work as head of the music department at NDR, he had legal training and had studied composition. He arrived, began work, and was triumphant. His first term in office lasted from 1959 to 1973, his second from 1985 to 1988.

Liebermann was possessed of an unparalleled—and in time, legendary—hunch for hidden potential in singers, conductors and directors. He put together an ensemble with the specific aim of making the house envied the world over. His programme aesthetics set new standards: he revered and revived the classics, but also created space for contemporary music, which he vigorously supported. And as a negotiating partner, Liebermann struck fear into the city's executive suites: when he came looking for money to realize his grand ideas, he was always a step ahead of the politicians or business people he dealt with.

In 1962, he managed to bring the veteran composer Igor Stravinsky to Hamburg for the celebrations of his eightieth birthday. In New York, Liebermann had heard a young tenor named Plácido Domingo, who went on to become a star and an audience favourite in the opera house on the Dammtor. In 1967, 50 years before the opening of the Elbphilharmonie, The New York Times said of Liebermann's Hamburg opera house: 'Now we know that there is something better than The Met.'

To recapture these glory days—albeit under today's different circumstances—will not be the work of the new riverside concert house and the NDR Elbphilharmonie Orchester alone. All of the city's ensembles, large and small, have a crucial role to play.

Hamburg's second great orchestra is now known as the 'Philharmonisches Staatsorchester Hamburg' or 'Hamburg Philharmonic', a very different institution to the NDR radio ensemble and with quite different objectives. The orchestra dates back to 1828, when it was founded by four middle-class music lovers. They wanted to give themselves and their own milieu something they regarded as indispensable: good

Above: the birthplace of Johannes Brahms in the Gängeviertel district.
Below: Brahms in the foyer of the Laeiszhalle, a marble sculpture by Max Klinger.

KENT NAGANO
CHIEF MUSIC DIRECTOR

Director Kent Nagano is quite familiar with new venues. During his tenure as conductor at the Opéra Nouvel in Lyon the building was gutted and the interior completely redesigned—only the facade was left intact. As principal conductor of the Orchestre symphonique de Montréal he inaugurated a newly constructed concert hall. These experiences will serve him well in his role as chief music director of the Hamburg Staatsoper and the Philharmonic State Opera. Audiences can look forward to exciting programmes with broad educational value, for which the Californian-born Nagano is famous.

concerts in which substantial musical works could be heard. Back then, there was no question of a truly democratic institution; they were not establishing a 'house for all', as the slogan of the Elbphilharmonie would later be. Nonetheless, the men had a typical no-nonsense Hamburg approach—no waiting around until local politicians woke up and did something. The four patrons compiled a list of subscribers for their planned 'Society for Staging Winter Concerts', drawn from their circle of acquaintances. The idea quickly took off. The first concert took place on 17 January 1829, mostly featuring musicians from the Stadt-Theater, forerunner of today's Staatsoper.

In the years that followed, the concerts became a fixture in Hamburg's music scene. Starting in 1855, the performances took place in what would later become the Conventgarten. But in 1886, competition from Berlin livened up the city's music business. A Berlin concert promoter sent the popular **Hans von Bülow** to Hamburg, bringing with him a specially-created orchestra, intended as direct competition to what was by now the 'Philharmonic Society', the successor to the original winter concerts, now conducted by Julius von Bernuth.

Competition between the two orchestras was fierce: by 1894, the Philharmonic Society was apparently considering complete capitulation, with plans afoot to dissolve the orchestra. Then Bülow, a huge audience favourite, died unexpectedly while on a trip to Egypt. Suddenly, the way was again clear for other orchestras. But the Philharmonic wisely decided to put its house in order: it created its own ensemble, so as to stop relying on musicians from here, there and everywhere. And so in 1896, the 'Association of Hamburg Friends of Music' was founded, supported by a mixture of public and private funds: for the first five years the Senate contributed 20,000 marks per season, on condition that one of the events would be a 'people's concert', charged at reasonable prices. In June 1908, it fell to the Philharmonic Orchestra to perform the inaugural concert of the new Laeiszhalle. In the years that followed, the Philharmonic's concerts cemented its place in the city's cultural life. Numerous virtuosos and conductors appeared as the guest performers, from violinist Fritz Kreisler to composer Richard Strauss.

In 1934, autonomy came to an abrupt halt. The Nazis merged the Philharmonic Orchestra with the Stadt-Theater Orchester, forming the Philharmonisches Staatsorchester, an ensemble intended for concert performances as well as for the needs of the opera house. Eugen Jochum was named the 'first general music director'. In 1945, like the country as a whole, the orchestra had to re-emerge from the depths of the abyss. In the early years of West Germany, the dominant figures on the conductor's podium were Joseph Keilberth and Wolfgang Sawallisch.

Flash-forward some decades and we find one of the most interesting eras in the orchestra's history, fascinating for its strongly-felt aesthetic contrasts. In 1997, the orchestra received a new general musical director, **Ingo Metzmacher**, renowned as a specialist in new and unusual music; during his term in office, he earned a reputation for productivity—and for a thick skin. Collaborating with director Peter Konwitschny, Metzmacher gave the Hamburg Philharmonic a distinctly new look and feel. Along the way, the duo not only made new friends, but also provided much musical food for thought. In their wake came the Australian **Simone Young**. From 2005 to 2015, Young served as both chief conductor of the Hamburg Philharmonic and artistic director of the Staatsoper. Her successor on the podium is now **Kent Nagano**, with Georges Delnon serving alongside him as artistic director.

'There's something happening in the world of music, and it's happening in Hamburg,' was Nagano's memorable phrase on his arrival. But whatever happens in Hamburg happens against a backdrop of its rich past. Introducing his first programme in April 2015, Nagano did not start by looking forward, preferring to reflect philosophically on tradition and quality. The Oper am Gänsemarkt, the first non-royal opera house on German soil, which entertained audiences nearby was built, the California-born composer reminded his German public, one hundred years before the founding of the United States. And what about Hamburg's Philharmonic Society? Begun in 1828, just a year after the death of Beethoven. It was a clever rhetorical debut.

For a city like Hamburg, having just two great orchestras might seem a little on the stingy side. So we also have the Hamburg Symphony Orchestra. By its own way of thinking, it is the city's real concert orchestra, since the NDR Orchester is defined by its origins on the radio, and the Philharmonic is above all the orchestra of the Staatsoper. Supported by its own patrons' society, the Hamburg Symphony Orchestra is a rather small orchestra, created by the merger of two even smaller ones. It was founded in 1957 under the name 'United Hamburg Orchestra'; in 1960, it incorporated the Hamburg Bach Orchestra, and took on its current name.

Existential crises, usually connected with budget shortfalls, loom large in the history of the Symphony Orchestra. But in 1975, when the Senate began a wave of cutbacks and demanded the dissolution of the orchestra, the ensemble's many tenacious supporters came out of the woodwork. Leonard Bernstein and Herbert von Karajan let it be known just how stupid they found any idea of closure. Patrons organized solidarity collections. In the end, abolition was scrapped, and the Symphony Orchestra was saved.

From 1995, the orchestra's artistic director was Peter Dannenberg, who put the orchestra on a stable footing for the future. He brought in the Russian conductor Andrey Boreyko, and later saw Daniel Kühnel take over as his successor. After Boreyko's departure, veteran English conductor **Jeffrey Tate** arrived on the scene at the start of the 2009–10 season, taking the helm for the wonderful adventure that is the Hamburg Symphony Orchestra. However, Tate's fame as a conductor could not prevent a familiar problem in 2013, as resurfacing budget issues yet again threatened catastrophe. In the end, the institution scraped through, just about. The city's department of culture ended up paying off the seven-figure deficit, not least because the demise of the orchestra expected to become the new resident orchestra at the Laeiszhalle would have cast a dark shadow over Hamburg's image as a musical city ahead of the Elbphilharmonie launch: the Symphony Orchestra is not only a great orchestra and an important musical institution, it is as tough as nails too.

A key player in the Hamburg concert scene is Hamburg Musik, a non-profit company run by Christoph Lieben-Seutter. In the years leading up to the opening of the Elbphilharmonie, this company has done much to prepare the way for the new concert hall. At times it has really had to dig new musical ground in Hamburg, under very trying circumstances. The company planned numerous concert series of its own, arranging collaborations with orchestras and other companies, looking to strengthen the programme of the Laeiszhalle while simultaneously preparing the ground for the Elbphilharmonie. That meant juggling many different interests, now with two concert halls under a single umbrella brand: no easy task.

On top, Hamburg still has a vibrant church-music scene, with a number of important organs and a rich and varied landscape of choirs. This musical environment nurtured the development of, among others, the chamber orchestra Hamburger Camerata.

The Hamburg Symphony Orchestra and its chief conductor Jeffrey Tate in the main hall of the Laeiszhalle, where the HSO is the orchestra-in-residence.

The forum of the Hochschule für Musik und Theater—sometimes known as the 'Alster Philharmonie', after one of Hamburg's interior lakes—has enough space for opera productions. The composer **György Ligeti** taught there. Hamburg resident **Alfred Schnittke** wrote ballet music to 'Peer Gynt' for John Neumeier's world-renowned ballet company. Within a stone's throw of the city, the composer **Sofia Gubaidulina** made her home in the tranquil village of Appen. **Paul Dessau**, a collaborator of Bertolt Brecht, was born close to St. Michaelis, as was **Berthold Goldschmidt**. Like Dessau, Goldschmidt had to flee from the Nazis. The composer **Peter Ruzicka** led the Staatsoper before becoming the director of the Salzburg Festival in 2001. For lovers of smaller ensembles, the Hamburg Friends of Chamber Music Society organizes guest performances by ensembles from all over the world.

In the early 1960s, the legendary clubs of St. Pauli were where The **Beatles** learned how to become true musical stars. Two decades later, 'Cats' helped transform Hamburg into a European capital of musical theatre. Soon, the spectrum of shows stretched from spectacular international productions like 'The Lion King' and 'Aladdin', to home-grown productions like 'Heiße Ecke' to alternative and experimental productions.

Local promoter **Karsten Jahnke** brings world stars to the city for stadium shows or more intimate open-air concerts in the Stadtpark. The Kampnagel theatre is regarded as a key space for experimental performances, serving equally well for concerts by piano hipster Chilly Gonzales as it does for an Elbphilharmonie avant-garde festival with the self-ironizing name 'Greatest Hits'. Then there are the other festivals, from the Reeperbahn Festival in the heart of entertainment-

The home of Ensemble Resonanz is the 'resonanzraum' in Hamburg's Feldstraße.
It is also the ensemble-in-residence in the Elbphilharmonie's Recital Hall.

addicted St. Pauli to the Dockville Festival in Wilhelmsburg. Decades of local pop music shouldn't be forgotten either. Clever boys in tracksuit tops (in bands like Tocotronic and Die Goldenen Zitronen) wrote so-called 'discourse pop' and were acclaimed as the 'Hamburg School' by equally clever music journalists. In the 1990s, **Jan Delay** came on the scene as one of the Absolute Beginners. German pop icon **Udo Lindenberg** has as important a place in Hamburg folklore, as does Heidi Kabel, the beloved local actress and singer who died in 2010. No account of Hamburg's musical life can miss out the traditional 'Pro Arte' concert series, which brought a long line of established stars to the Laeiszhalle stage in the years before the new concert house was conceived. Since autumn 2014, a small Off-Elbphilharmonie has lurked where you might least expect it: in an old bunker next to the stadium of F.C. St. Pauli.

This 'resonanzraum' concert space, close to the Reeperbahn, is the fulfilment of the dream of the democratically-organized string chamber orchestra **Ensemble Resonanz**. It took a few years for the ensemble to play its way onto the musical map of Hamburg. A board of ten private patrons donated a total of €200,000 to convert the new location, city taxpayers chipped in matching funds, and the rest of the money came from a variety of foundations. The design of the space, with its metre-thick walls, is hip but pleasingly unpretentious. And there's a well-stocked bar. In the Elbphilharmonie, the Resonanz team will become ensemble-in-residence. In January 2017, they will be the first ensemble to play the Recital Hall. This parade of the city's musical diversity highlights the living landscape in which our great new hall now takes its place. And all of this only in Hamburg.

PROF. BARBARA KISSELER
SENATOR OF CULTURE

When she assumed office in 2011 the theatre
scholar inherited a difficult situation: the
construction of the Elbphilharmonie was stalled,
quarrels had broken out between those responsible
for the project, and the undertaking was repeatedly
plagued by bad news of soaring costs and missed
deadlines. All hopes were pinned on Barbara
Kisseler, whose task seemed near to impossible.
Together with First Mayor Olaf Scholz, however,
Kisseler succeeded in placing the project on a solid
contractual foundation. If a selection of significant
quotes from the evolutionary history of the
Elbphilharmonie is ever collected, Barbara
Kisseler's command, 'No more messing about!',
encapsulates the new momentum that the
independent Senator for Culture brought
to the project.

Finale

The home stretch.

Tension and anticipation.

A day in the life of the
Elbphilharmonie.

WOW! THEY ACTUALLY WENT AND BUILT IT

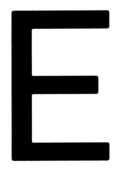arly in 2016 the final sprint got under way, as 11 January 2017 began to loom ever closer. And increasingly, the mood of the city began to shift. Looking back, early May seems to have been the moment when a new, joyful chord appeared in the symphony of public opinion: the day the online lottery for 900 free tickets for the opening concert opened, and the sheer number of enquiries collapsed the servers. In the end, there were a total of 223,346 applications from 73 different countries. Finally, the words of then First Mayor Ole von Beust, back in April 2007, were proven right: 'We're not bluffing—it's really happening'. The servers collapsed a second time in mid-June, when tickets went on general sale. By this time, almost every retailer of Elbphilharmonie concerts had sold out their subscriptions. Gone like hotcakes, in no time at all.

During the presentation of the opening season's programme, First Mayor Olaf Scholz was proud and relieved to draw a clear line under the troubles of the past: Hamburg has suffered long enough, he said. For the opening festival, several weeks long, general director Christoph Lieben-Seutter planned a special highlight: he booked the legendary avant-garde rock band Einstürzende Neubauten for the newly-built Grand Hall—a wryly ironic gesture, since the group's name translates as 'Collapsing New Buildings'. Tickets for the band's evening concert sold out so fast that an additional afternoon gig was soon added.

There were plenty more signs of excitement and anticipation. In City Hall, a deal on running costs for the Elbphilharmonie and the Laeiszhalle was agreed: €6 million per year, and another €5 million in start-up funding, every year for the first four years. Not outrageous sums by international concert-hall standards. Ten years previously, they had reckoned very cautiously upon €3.2 million per year.

After the installation of the 'white skin', Culture Senator Barbara Kisseler raved about the building's architecture, saying: 'So overwhelming, it doesn't even need the music'. The Grand Hall was handed over to the city on 30 June: on time, without fuss and without publicity. There was no need for it: the project was simply moving ahead as planned, on schedule, without pausing to draw breath. And at this stage, it was important that nothing get in the way of the building inspections. By now, these were proceeding full-tilt, with experts examining every inch of the building, checking to see that everything was in place and working as it should.

The NDR Elbphilharmonie Orchester prepared to move out of its existing rehearsal spaces, in the NDR radio complex, and into its brand new home. The first rehearsals in the building, a first chance to see how things would work day-to-day. Excitement was growing now, at all levels of society.

The Elbphilharmonie is an exciting new Hamburg landmark, ready to be discovered by the city's inhabitants and to be taken into their hearts. The glass wave atop the old brick building is set to become an international icon, a symbol of Germany's place as a leading cultural nation, just as iconic as the Eiffel Tower for Paris, or the Sydney Opera House for the whole of Australia.

We're not bluffing—it's really happening. Really? The best answer to this question is to make the short journey along Hafenstraße, from Fischmarkt in the direction of the city centre. On your left, the Reeperbahn in all its glory, on your right, the famous tower of St. Michaelis. Even before you pass the St. Pauli Piers, the Elbphilharmonie appears on the horizon of the port. In good weather it gives off a warm glow; in any weather it is unique and inviting. And all you can really think is: Wow! They actually went and built it.

Prelude: chief conductor
Thomas Hengelbrock at the first
rehearsals in early September
with the NDR Elbphilharmonie
Orchester in the Grand Hall.
Among the composers played that
day: Brahms and Mendelssohn,
both from Hamburg.

Tutti: the orchestra-in-residence of the Elbphilharmonie in harmony with itself and its new musical home.

The most exciting jobs in the world
of classical music are to be found
on the stage of the Grand Hall of the
Elbphilharmonie.

Queen of the Night: the
Elbphilharmonie seems
to borrow its lustre from
the moon.

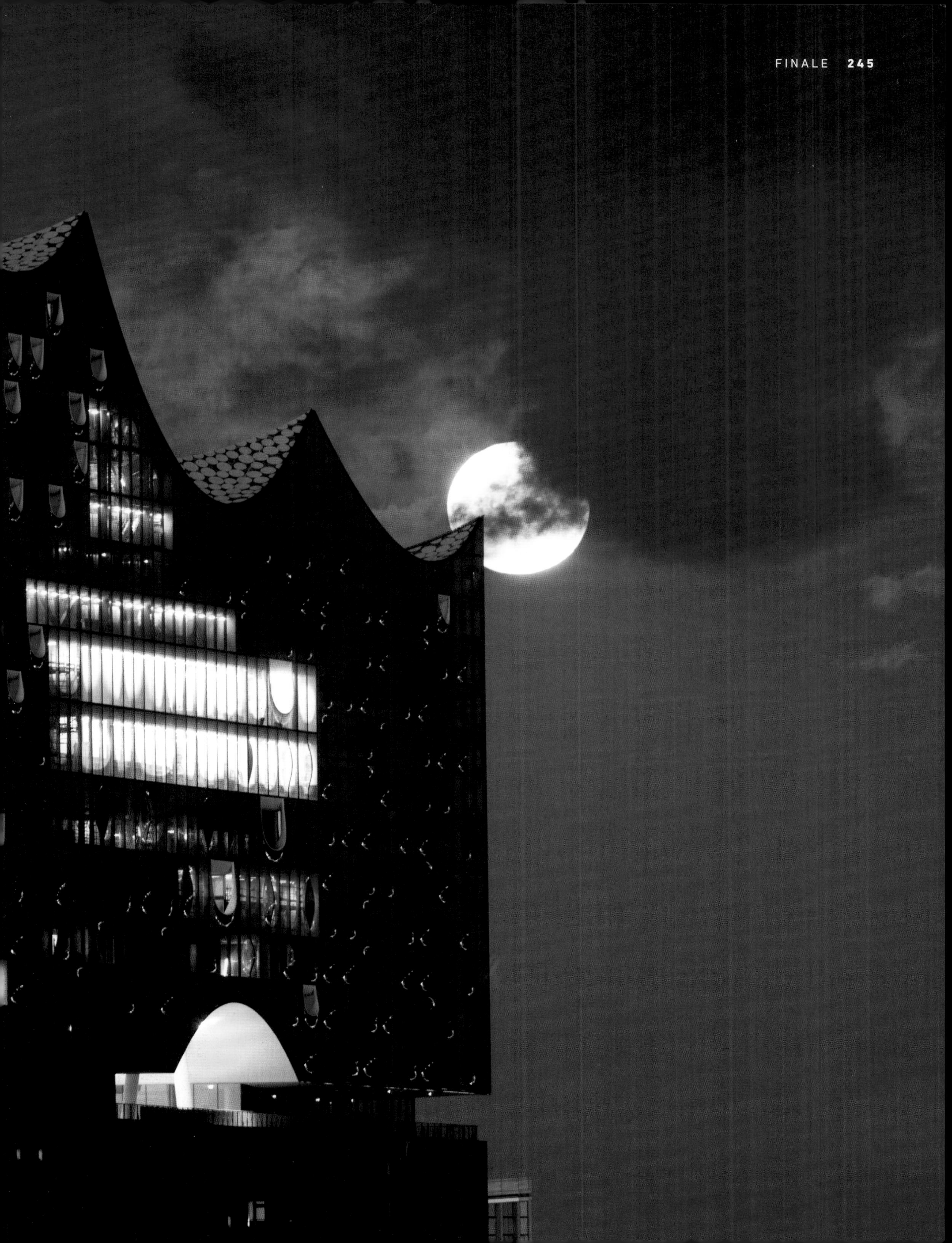

JOACHIM MISCHKE

studied music, journalism and English. He is the chief cultural reporter with the Hamburger Abendblatt newspaper. His journalistic passions include all aspects of Hamburg's cultural and musical life. He has covered the building of the Elbphilharmonie right from the start. The author of numerous books, including 'Hamburg Musik!' (2008), he is also a member of the jury for the German Record Critics' Award.

MICHAEL ZAPF

born in 1965, has been photographing his home town of Hamburg for 32 years. His photographs have appeared in newspapers, magazines and books. He has published numerous photography books on Hamburg and the north of Germany.

We are grateful to the Department of Culture of the City of Hamburg, to HamburgMusik gGmbH and to Herzog & de Meuron for their professional expertise and unstinting support.

TEXT AND IDEA: Joachim Mischke

PHOTOS: Michael Zapf

CONCEPT, EDITORIAL, DESIGN
BEHNKEN&PRINZ
Infographic: Jelka Lerche

ENGLISH EDITION
Dorit Aurich
English Translation: Büro LS Anderson

PROJECT COORDINATION
Dr. Marten Brandt

PUBLISHING HOUSE
EDEL BOOKS
AN IMPRINT OF EDEL GERMANY GMBH

COPYRIGHT © 2016 EDEL GERMANY GMBH,
Neumühlen 17, 22763 Hamburg
www.edel.com
2nd print run 2016

LITHOGRAPHY
Edelweiß-Publish
www.edelweiss-publish.de

PRINTING AND BINDING
optimal media GmbH
Glienholzweg 7, 17207 Röbel/Müritz

PHOTO CREDITS

All photographs © Michael Zapf

Pages 40, 59, 62, 66: © 2016, Herzog & de Meuron Basel; Page 49: PR Harpa; Page 51: KKL Luzern
Page 52: Lauterbach/Berliner Philharmoniker; Page 53: William Beaucardet; Page 54: Markus Hanke/VISUM
Page 63: www.breuel-bild.de; Page 121: Stefan Thomas Kroeger/laif
Pages 132-133: © Herzog & de Meuron/Elbphilharmonie und Laeiszhalle Service GmbH, Grafik: bloomimages
Page 168: Christian O. Bruch/laif; Page 208: Vintage Germany
Page 211: Staatsarchiv Hamburg (2); Hamburgische Staatsoper, www.hamburg-bildarchiv.de; Page 214: Staatsarchiv Hamburg
Page 215: Laeiszhalle; Pages 216-217: hhla.de/hamburger-fotoarchiv.de
Page 219: Staatsarchiv Hamburg, hamburger-fotoarchiv.de, @ Zoch; Page 222: NDR/Henriette Bandulik
Page 224: NDR/NWDR, INTERFOTO/Lebrecht Music Collection/David Farrell, imago/CTK Photo; Page 229: ullstein bild
Page 232: © J. Konrad Schmidt (BFF Professional); Page 233: Ensemble Resonanz, Tobias Schult
Page 234: Johannes Arlt; Page 246: Svenja Zapf

Printed in Germany
ISBN 978-3-8419-0481-2
WG 1960

BIBLIOGRAPHY / SOURCES
(SELECTION)

Books

Briegleb, Till: „Eine Vision wird Wirklichkeit – auf historischem Grund: Die Elbphilharmonie entsteht" Murmann, Hamburg 2007.

Cornehl, Ulrich: „Raummassagen. Der Architekt Werner Kallmorgen (1902–1979)" Dölling & Galitz, Hamburg 2003.

Essmeyer, Sonja: „Hamburger Konzertstätten von der Mitte des 18. bis Anfang des 20. Jahrhunderts vor dem Hintergrund der Entwicklung des öffentlichen Hamburger Konzertwesens". Master's thesis Angewandte Kulturwissenschaften, University of Lüneburg, Lüneburg 1996.

Freundeskreis der Laeiszhalle (ed.): „Zurück in die Zukunft. Musikhalle Hamburg, Kleiner Saal. Ein Projekt zum rekonstruktiven Wiederaufbau". Hamburg 2002.

Freundeskreis der Elbphilharmonie & Laeiszhalle (ed.): „Ein magischer Ort. Hamburg freut sich auf die Elbphilharmonie". Schümann Verlag, Hamburg 2011.

Gimpel, Lenhard: „Zur Akustik früher Konzertstätten in Hamburg". Master's thesis Audiokommunikation, TU Berlin, Berlin 2008.

Hofmann, Kurt: „Johannes Brahms und Hamburg. Neue Erkenntnisse zu einem alten Thema". Dialog, Reinbek 1986.

Hornbostel, Wilhelm / Klemm, David (ed.): „Martin Haller. Leben und Werk 1835-1925". Dölling und Galitz, München / Hamburg 1997.

Jaacks, Gisela (ed.): „300 Jahre Oper in Hamburg. 1678-1978". Museum für Hamburgische Geschichte / Vereins- und Westbank, Hamburg 1978.

Kleßmann, Eckart: „Georg Philipp Telemann". Ellert & Richter, Hamburg 2004.

Kornemann, Matthias: „Johannes Brahms". Ellert & Richter, Hamburg 2006.

Laeiszhalle – Musikhalle Hamburg (ed.): „100 Jahre Laeiszhalle – Musikhalle Hamburg. Geschichte, Menschen, Sternstunden". Hamburg 2008.

Lipski, Thomas: „Von der Tonhalle bis zur Elbphilharmonie. Konzertsaalorgeln in Hamburg", in: „organ – Journal für die Orgel". Schott, Mainz 2005.

Mischke, Joachim: „Hamburg Musik!" Hoffmann und Campe, Hamburg 2008.

Sittard, Josef: „Geschichte des Musik- und Concertwesens in Hamburg vom 14. Jahrhundert bis auf die Gegenwart". Altona and Leipzig, 1890.

Articles

„Wunschkonzert. Wie aus einer genialen Idee der größte Bauskandal in Hamburgs Historie wurde. Die unglaubliche Geschichte der Elbphilharmonie. Eine Dokumentation von Andreas Dey, Jan Haarmeyer und Joachim Mischke" Hamburger Abendblatt, 13 December 2013.

Other printed matter, etc.

Böttcher, Ingo / Hackbusch, Norbert: „Kostenexplosions-Ursachenforschung. Ein Fazit zum ersten Untersuchungsausschuss Elbphilharmonie". Die Linke, Fraktion in der Hamburgischen Bürgerschaft. Hamburg, 2011.

Senats-Drucksache 17/3924: „Errichtung eines ‚Maritimen Kultur- und Erlebnisbausteins' und einer ‚Neuen Konzerthalle' in der HafenCity". 16 December 2003.

Senats-Drucksache 17/4256: „Betr.: Philharmonie auf Kaispeicher A". 11 February 2004.

Senats-Drucksache 18/2570: „Realisierung des Projekts Elbphilharmonie". 12 July 2005.

Senats-Drucksache 18/3017: „Realisierung des Projekts Elbphilharmonie". 25 October 2005.

Senats-Drucksache 18/5526: „Realisierung des Projekts Elbphilharmonie". 19 December 2006.

Senats-Drucksache 18/6278: „Realisierung des Projekts Elbphilharmonie. Information zur Notwendigkeit der Erhöhung des Bürgschaftsrahmens von 153 um 5 auf bis zu 140 Mio. Euro und zur Konkretisierung der Zeitplanung". 22 May 2007.

Senats-Drucksache 19/1841: „Realisierung des Projekts Elbphilharmonie. Sachstandsbericht zum 23. Dezember 2008 und Ergänzung des Haushaltsplan-Entwurfs 2009/2010 zur Finanzierung von Mehrkosten". 23 December 2008.

Senats-Drucksache 20/7738: „Realisierung des Projekts Elbphilharmonie. Bericht über die Neuordnung des Projekts Elbphilharmonie. Nachbewilligung von Haushaltsmitteln im Haushaltsplan 2013/2014". 23 April 2013

Senats-Drucksache 21/2839: „Fortgeschriebenes Nutzungskonzept für den laufenden Spielbetrieb von Elbphilharmonie und Laeiszhalle nach der Eröffnungsphase; Betrieb der öffentlichen Plaza; Planungen zur Inbetriebnahme und Eröffnung der Elbphilharmonie und Aktivierung der Musikstadt". 12 January 2016.

„Thesen zur Kostenexplosion Elbphilharmonie". Bündnis 90 / Die Grünen, Fraktion in der Hamburgischen Bürgerschaft. Hamburg, 2013.

Author's acknowledgement:
My greatest thanks go to Sabine Hengesbach: for everything, and much more.